Dear Reader:

The book you are about to read is the latest bestseller from St. Martin's True Crime Library, the imprint *The New York Times* calls "the leader in true crime!" Each month, we offer you a fascinating account of the latest, most sensational crime that has captured the national attention. St. Martin's is the publisher of perennial best-selling true crime author Jack Olsen (SON and DOC) whose SALT OF THE EARTH is the true story of how one woman fought and triumphed over life-shattering violence; Joseph Wambaugh called it "powerful and absorbing." DEATH OF A LITTLE PRINCESS recounts the investigation into the horrifying murder of child beauty queen JonBenét Ramsey; the author is Carlton Smith. Fannie Weinstein and Melinda Wilson tell the story of a beautiful honors student who was lured into the dark world of sex for hire in THE COED CALL GIRL MURDER.

St. Martin's True Crime Library gives you the stories *behind* the headlines. Our authors take you right to the scene of the crime and into the minds of the most notorious murderers to show you what really makes them tick. St. Martin's True Crime Library paperbacks are better than the most terrifying thriller, because it's all true! The next time you want a crackling good read, make sure it's got the St. Martin's True Crime Library logo on the spine—you'll be up all night!

Charles E. Spicer, Jr.
Senior Editor, St. Martin's True Crime Library

IT COULDN'T HAPPEN IN
MY TOWN . . .

The teenagers had gathered late at night in a park in Eugene, Oregon. One of the boys, Wayde Hudson, pressed the release on the stopwatch and shouted, "Go!"

Lisa Fentress jumped into a circle of white middle-class teenagers. As the circle closed in on Lisa, she was pounded on all sides by fists and feet. Hudson kept looking at his stopwatch. His gang leader had told him that a proper *jumping in*, or gang-initiation ceremony, lasted a precise time, specifically seventy-four seconds. When seventy-four seconds were up, he shouted, "Stop!"

"Welcome to the Seventy-Four Hoover Crips," Hudson shouted triumphantly. He handed her a blue bandanna. Whenever she wore it, it would signify her gang membership . . .

And now Lisa was also given the job of pressing a button on a guy. Put another way, Lisa's job was to finger a guy to be murdered. And since it was being done to maintain gang unity and loyalty, there was nothing wrong with that.

Was there?

GANG MOM

FRED ROSEN

St. Martin's Paperbacks

GANG MOM

Copyright © 1998 by Fred Rosen.

Cover photograph by Chris Pietsch.

ISBN: 0-312-96810-8

Printed in the United States of America

St. Martin's Paperbacks edition / December 1998

10 9 8 7 6 5 4 3 2 1

For my Uncle Izzie and summer
afternoons together in the
bleachers at Yankee Stadium

A WORD ABOUT SOURCES

The story began as an article in the June 1997 issue of *Reader's Digest*. But as with any article, there is never enough space. I didn't get to explore the gang phenomenon as in-depth as I wanted to. Thus the book you hold in your hand.

The story you are about to read is true. Some names have been changed to protect the privacy of those involved who were on the periphery of the case. Also, whenever possible, the names of underage gang members have been changed. All name changes appear initially in italics.

Interviews, official documents, including wiretaps, warrants, statements to police, as well as excerpts of official trial transcripts and indigenous news accounts, have all been used in the writing of this book.

A few scenes have been presented out of chronological order not for dramatic effect, but to simplify the narrative. Likewise, the "Gang Mom" investigation involved many police officers and for the sake of clarity, the story is presented principally through the eyes of the two lead cops.

"And thus I clothe my naked villainy with old, odd ends . . . and seem a saint when most I play the devil."
William Shakespeare, *Richard III*

PROLOGUE

CLEVELAND, OHIO, 1976

IT HAD BEEN A gathering of bikers, outlaws who reveled in free sex and violence. Mary Fockler had been there and had a great time and when it was time to go home, she didn't want the party to end. So her roommate drove her to a biker clubhouse. Her goal was to have a good time.

Fockler was a very attractive woman, tall and well-built. She had piercing blue eyes that seemed to go right through you. They gave her a special, almost charismatic air. But all that was irrelevant to the bikers. They wanted sex, pure and simple, and as long as Fockler didn't look like Godzilla, it was going to be a rather pleasant late afternoon.

If Fockler had one particular peccadillo, it was an insane love of animals. You know the type; they think of animals as little human beings, only with a lot more hair. Which was why Fockler took her dog with her wherever she went. Even over to a Hells Angels clubhouse for sex, drugs and rock and roll.

While she was having sex with the bikers, Fockler's dog got into a disagreement with a biker's mutt. Fockler happened to glance over and noticed that her dog was losing the fight. In panic lest her "snookums" should die, she ran out into the street half clad.

Police arrived and Fockler now claimed the bikers raped her. Fockler's case was taken up by the media. The image of a half-naked woman running through the streets of Cleveland shouting, "I was raped, I was raped," was too good to be true. The burgeoning women's movement, seeing the perfect poster child for the cause of abused women everywhere in the plight of "poor" Mary Fockler, took her case to its collective bosom. They pressed the police for immediate action.

Police brought in thirty-two of the bikers for questioning. Thirteen were eventually arrested, and Fockler identified five of the thirteen as the men who raped her. A trial was set..

Almost immediately, rumors began swirling through the Cleveland underground that the accused men actually belonged to a rival motorcycle gang, not the one Fockler associated with, and that she was just "getting them."

Before the trial, Fockler was drinking in a bar when a uniformed cop happened to enter. His name was *Jules Sampson.* Joking around, Fockler went up to him and said, "Where were you when I needed you?"

Because one of the accused was a close friend of Sampson's, he doubted her story. But Sampson was young and inexperienced and apparently would do anything for a friend. He told her that maybe something could be done about the situation. Fockler said all she wanted to do was blow town and start a new life.

Sampson figured the bikers would pay her to drop the charges. There would be nothing wrong with that, Sampson reasoned, because she was lying anyway. But by that time, Fockler was enjoying all the attention she was getting. She was an impressionable woman who, for the first time in her life, was the center of attention. And she craved more.

Ever the "honest" woman, Fockler told police that Sampson approached *her* and offered her a bribe. Internal affairs cops put a tap on her phone. When she called Sampson, they discussed a grand and a plane ticket out of town in return for Fockler dropping charges. Sampson was eventually fired.

That was one man Fockler had brought down. One down and five to go. But Fockler wasn't done with her con job. Not just yet.

At the trial, Fockler dressed for the occasion in bright, loose clothes instead of her usual tight leathers. The women's movement had suggested the change so the jury would think of her as younger and more virginal. The prosecution, who sincerely believed Fockler's story, did not hesitate to call her to the stand. After recounting the alleged rape, it was defending attorney Rocco Russo's turn to question her.

Russo had discovered that Fockler had a very interesting tattoo which he brought to the jury's attention. When he asked Fockler to reveal it, she shyly opened the top of her blouse. There, for the jury to see, was a tattoo of a butterfly above her breast. The jury reasoned that the tattoo didn't go with the image of the cute little girl, a supposition confirmed when Russo produced ten men who had watched as she was tattooed.

When it was the defense's turn, Russo's key witness was Fockler's married sister Judy who testified that Fockler had, from an early age, been a habitual liar. She explained to the jury that the only reason she agreed to testify for the defense was because she was determined to have her sister get help for her problems.

"My sister is excited about her new-found fame," Judy testified. "She calls me at noon from the court-house phone and tells me she's going to be famous," Judy said. "She's going to be on the Johnny Carson show."

Helluva surprise for Johnny.

When the five men were found not guilty of raping Mary Fockler, their fellow bikers rose as one and ap-plauded the jury, while demanding justice be dispensed to the woman who had maligned them all. The judge, disgusted at the whole proceeding, released the defen-dants and banged down his gavel to close the proceed-ings.

Mary Fockler had had a rapid rise to fame and an even more rapid fall. It had been heady in that rarefied atmo-sphere where everyone listened to her and she was the star attraction. So what if she'd lied? She'd gotten the attention, hadn't she? She'd almost put the con over. But now that she had been discredited, it was time to leave town.

Fockler felt that her greatest fame still lay in front of her. After all, she hadn't made Johnny's show yet, had she?

ONE

Burning Season

ONE

SEPTEMBER 24, 1994

IT WAS THE FIRST day of burning season and fires blazed all around Eugene, Oregon.

Jim Michaud stood at the front door of his rustic home on the outskirts of the city. As he sipped a martini, he thought back to the many burning seasons of his youth, when his father would set the barrels up outside their home, fill them with anything that needed burning, and set them on fire. Their neighbors would be doing the same thing, so a ring of controlled fire would encircle their neighborhood.

Burning season was the beginning of fall, a time to burn your detritus. Michaud liked to think that it was also an opportunity to burn from memory any sins committed against others, an opportunity to create a slate that was clean and purified by fire.

Some might consider such existential thoughts to be unusual for a country boy like Michaud. A true Westerner, he had grown up in the backwoods of Oregon where he hunted and fished, first as a child, then as an adolescent and now as a forty-one-year-old adult. Yet he was anything but a backwoodsman.

That martini in his hand, for instance. Most guys he

knew at work preferred a beer. His taste, though, ran to something a little more refined. He took a sip of the drink, made with Bombay gin and dry Martini & Rossi vermouth, then looked out at the fires again.

This time, the fires made him think about a pig roast he and Paula had thrown when they'd moved in last year. They had invited all their friends over, used a backhoe to dig a pit and filled it with white-hot charcoal and then added the pièce de résistance, a full-size pig. The poor sucker was covered with earth and left to roast its guts out until later in the day when it was dug up and dug into. But again, Michaud was a man of contrasts. Pig roasts might be fun once every ten years, but he liked to cook more sophisticated dishes like beef bourguignon, adding the spices carefully on the "island" that stood in the kitchen of his home.

He looked down at his watch and pressed the dial that made it light up in that bright turquoise color that was all the rage now. It said 11:17. Time for bed. He liked to get into work early, before anyone else arrived.

Turning, he walked through french doors into the kitchen, then through the living room with its projection TV. Except for the modern appliances like the TV, the house might as well have been in Montana, decorated as it was with wooden beams and wooden flooring, Plains Indian blankets and Plains Indian art.

Michaud walked into the second bedroom on the left, furnished with a queen-size bed and two dressers. The room looked lived-in, with things out of place, sort of comfortable and confused at the same time.

Draped over a chair beside his bed was a cross-hatched shoulder holster. It was a lateral draw, so the butt of his .45mm Sig Sauer automatic faced out, affording a quick, easy draw. On the front straps were a shiny lawman's star and a beeper.

He slipped into bed beside his sleeping fiancée Paula and heard the steady sing-song of her breath, in and out, in and out. He paused for a moment, contemplating her beautiful form beneath the sheets, and then put his hand on her, slowly caressing. Soon, she turned toward him and they intertwined.

Too many times, Michaud had been in the middle of making love when murder intervened. He hoped this would not be one of them.

The teenagers, who had gathered late at night in a park in the city, could see the flames from scattered fires. As they smelled the odor of leaves and other things burning, *Wayde Hudson* pressed the release on the stopwatch and shouted, "Go!"

Lisa Fentress jumped into a circle of white middle-class teenagers who had gathered in a deserted lot on the outskirts of Eugene. As the circle closed in on Lisa, she was pounded on all sides by fists and feet. Hudson kept looking at his stopwatch. His gang leader had told him that Lisa should go first, and that a proper *jumping in*, or gang-initiation ceremony, lasted a precise time, specifically seventy-four seconds. When seventy-four seconds were up, he shouted, "Stop!"

The gang members, Joe, Jim, Angel, *Larry*, *Wayde*, *Linda*, *Jack*, *Cameron*, *Jasmine*, *Lennie*, and *Robert*, all drew back. Lisa lay bruised and bloody, a cut across her bottom lip, her eyes already swelling shut.

"Welcome to the Seventy-four Hoover Crips," Hudson shouted triumphantly. He handed her a blue *rag*, actually a bandanna. Whenever she wore it, it would signify her gang membership because blue was the "official" gang color. "Lisa, you're now a full-fledged member of the gang," Hudson shouted. With that, the videotape recorder that had been brought to record the event was turned off.

The gang leader had told Wayde Hudson that there was a difference between mixing in and jumping in as a means of entry into a gang.

"*Jumping in* means that the gang beats you up until they consider you to be sufficiently beaten to be a member of the gang. *Mixing in* means taking the fall for somebody who is a gang member. If you take the rap for them and they avoid being prosecuted for something they've done, then you're mixed in."

Few if any of the 74 Hoover Crips had had prior gang experience, and therefore never questioned their gang leader's definitions. Had they, they would have discovered that there was actually no difference between mixing in and jumping in, that they were in fact the same thing.

The gang Lisa had joined was a bunch of punk-ass white kids, high school dropouts who thought that, because they banded together and took the name of a black street gang that controlled part of southeast Los Angeles, they were cool.

These were kids who, while they may not have grown up with silver spoons in their mouths, knew nothing of poverty, nothing of discrimination because of skin color and, most importantly, nothing of manipulation by a gang leader. They were not cynical, tired beyond their years from exposure to constant street violence, the type of kids who knew a con man when they saw one. They were kids, with time on their hands, looking for the thrill that violence affords, something exciting enough to get their blood going when they weren't stoned or drunk.

Like most middle-class kids who join gangs, Lisa felt alienated from her peers. As long as she remembered, she had always hated kids. *They were always so mean to me growing up*, she thought. *And when I got older, all the girls wanted to do was talk about their boyfriends.*

As for her home life, it was nothing if not strained. She felt impotent at home, at the mercy of her parents' whims, never free to assert herself, to be her own woman. The gang gave her the one thing she lacked. Power. People knew who she was. They wouldn't mess with her because she was a member of the 74 Hoover Crips. It was kind of like she, Wayde, Larry and all the rest had formed their own *family*.

What a wonderful feeling, that sense of belonging, of being part of something greater than yourself! Lisa Fentress cherished that feeling more than anything. It was a feeling unlike any other, a feeling so heady, so strong, so intoxicating that in order not to lose it, she was willing to chuck the belief system she had grown up with, that some things were wrong and some things were right absolutely. She decided that, for her gang, she would dwell in the gray area, neither wrong nor right, just what was right for the gang regardless of the consequences. That was why she readily agreed to become a *button woman*.

She was given the job of pressing a button on a guy. Put another way, Lisa's job was to finger a guy to be murdered. And since it was being done to maintain gang unity and loyalty, there was nothing wrong with that.

Was there?

TWO

HAD IT NOT BEEN for Meriwether Lewis, the Eugene chapter of the 74 Hoover Crips would not have had a turf to begin with. It was Lewis who, in 1806, explored the Willamette River Valley during his fabled expedition to find the Northwest Passage. In the process, he made peace with the Indians who inhabited the valley.

Not much changed in the years immediately after he left to return to Virginia, but the mere fact that he and his partner William Clark and their Corps of Discovery had penetrated the area opened it up to white trappers and hunters, who would go on to make fortunes off the abundant wildlife that inhabited the area, and would inexorably affect the history of the United States.

The valley was so fertile that almost two centuries later, there were sections that were almost as pristine as in Lewis and Clark's day. But there were also the trappings of modern civilization, most notably the University of Oregon that made its home in this major northwest city, where Indians walk the streets harmoniously with cowboys, and gun shops coexist with head shops. It's the Old West and the 1960's all rolled into one.

Nestled snugly in Oregon's Willamette River Valley, Eugene is a tight-knit, secure community. But it has one major source of vulnerability to the corruption of the outside world.

The town sits on the Interstate 5 corridor, a major thoroughfare to Portland in the north, and California to the south. Because of its proximity to these population centers, Eugene is susceptible to urban problems. Like gangs.

Lisa Fentress admired the au courant gang look—baggy clothing in dull colors. But the school she attended felt just the opposite. The admistration believed that wearing gang clothing incited gang-type violence. The school passed an ordinance banning students from dressing as "gangsters." In protest, Lisa led a walkout among students, who, like her, believed in freedom of clothing. Not to be outdone, the school punished her by forcing her to attend a gang-prevention seminar at the Downtown Athletic Club run by the community's dynamic anti-gang activist, Mary Thompson.

Mary Thompson had exploded on the Eugene scene like a comet in the night sky. She had lived in anonymity for years, she said, but when organized gangs first came to Eugene in 1991, she decided to take action.

Her son Beau had been seduced by the power of gangs. A small, tousle-haired kid, he looked innocent enough to be in one of those milk ads. But Beau was hardly an innocent. Barely thirteen years old, he helped form the 74 Hoover Crips, taking the gang name "Bishop," and subsequently served time in the Mac-Laren Juvenile Facility for gang-related crimes.

Instead of fretting like most would, Mary Thompson became an anti-gang activist. Her message was simple: "If it could happen to my family, it could happen to yours."

She began conducting anti-gang seminars at high schools and youth centers, where she spoke passionately to teenagers of the good life her son Beau gave up, of her pain in watching him go down the wrong road. She showed students her photo albums filled with heart-warming shots of Beau proudly wearing his Cub Scout uniform, fishing with his father, and opening presents on Christmas Day like any normal American kid. But he wasn't any normal American kid, Mary said, not since he got involved with gangs.

Instead of the scenes depicted in the photographs, in her mind's eye she saw Beau selling guns at a local ice cream shop, serving time in prison, and threatening cops with a revolver. She saw a boy who, ever since he became "Bishop," had a gaze as hard as glacial ice and a heart frozen with hate for authority.

As her stature in the community increased, so did her influence. She formed a close relationship with the police department. Law enforcement looked to Mary as the one person who could break the spell that gangs cast over the city's youth. She formed a close working relationship with Ric Raynor, a detective in the anti-gang unit. Eventually, the department appointed her to the newly formed Gang Prevention Task Force.

Like the best evangelists, Mary could spellbind a crowd with the emotion behind her words, her commitment to keeping Eugene gang-free, her zeal in allowing the city's children to keep their childhood pristine. And Mary vowed publicly to continue to pursue her cause, to break the hold of gangs in Eugene, to stop kids from joining them, as long as one breath remained in her body.

As Lisa listened to Mary tell her story, she felt very moved and attended a subsequent meeting of the Gang Prevention Task Force that Mary was a part of. It was there that she met Aaron Iturra.

"Hi, is Aaron there?" said Lisa into the phone. She was in the privacy of her room at home and took a quick toke of the joint in her free hand.

"Uh, he's busy right now, but if you want—"

"No, it's okay. Never mind," Lisa interrupted, and hung up. Taking another toke, she made her second call.

"He's home," she said. "I just talked to his sister."

"Good. Now call James."

The third call was to James "Jim" Elstad.

"It's a 'go,' " she said.

The wind came whistling in through the window of the back bedroom, where Janyce Iturra lay sleeping. Despite the weather, Janyce always slept with her windows open. She liked the feeling of fresh air around her. She worked hard during the day, as a receiving clerk at Fred Myers, a large department store. And since she usually went to work at four or five, she was in bed by nine.

When the phone rang at ten, it woke her up. She heard her daughter Maya go out to get Aaron because the phone call was for him. After he came back in, she heard him say:

"Well, who is it, Maya?"

"I don't know," Maya answered. "It was just a girl. She hung up."

Janyce drifted back to sleep.

Minutes later, seventeen-year-old "Crazy" Joe Brown stood in front of the Iturra home. The house was a panhandle, situated in back of another, the two connected by a narrow alley. The beauty of it was, you couldn't see the panhandle house from the street. This type of dwelling was common in Eugene.

Brown was a short kid who, at five-foot-six, weighed all of 140 pounds soaking wet. Dressed in black shirt and pants, with jet-black hair, scraggly mustache and goatee, he cased the joint. Quickly, he realized he had come too early. The house was lit up. People inside were still awake. He left and returned around midnight.

This time, the house was dark. He tapped the glass of the living-room window several times just to be sure. When no one answered, he walked back to the far end of the alley where Jim Elstad crouched in the darkness.

"Iturra's asleep," he whispered, the cool night air making his breath come out in a white plume.

Elstad nodded and followed Brown back to the house. Both boys were dressed in the gang colors: blue bandannas over their faces and heads, blue bandannas covering their hands. Their gang leader had told Elstad and Brown that the open display of their gang colors was a symbol that someone was going to get killed. This was ritualized behavior. Dressing in this manner signified this as a Crip event, a Crip killing. Their gang leader had assured them that their "brother" Crips in Portland and Los Angeles would soon know about their work.

They lifted the door of the garage, and found themselves standing before a bedroom that had been partitioned off by sheet rock in the rear. Brown pushed at the door of the makeshift room.

Clothes, beer bottles, soda cans and empty pizza boxes were strewn all over the floor. On a small dresser made of cheap pressed wood were various types of shaving lotion and high school loose-leaf binders filled to bursting. There was also an old console color TV set.

Two of the walls were decorated with posters celebrating Motley Crue, Menace II Society and Budweiser beer. There were pictures of two attractive young women dressed in low-cut outfits revealing their cleavage. The two other walls of the bedroom were covered in graffiti.

And there on the bed was the target, Aaron Iturra, sleeping arm in arm with his girlfriend Carrie Barkley.

Brown shook Aaron's bare back. The teenager continued to slumber, but then Brown saw Iturra move his head a little bit, and start to get up. By then, Jim Elstad was at the door, holding a .45 caliber Smith & Wesson revolver in his right hand. Steadying it with his left, Elstad raised the weapon.

Brown reached down to the girl's purse, which sat on the floor amid the litter of the beer bottles and pizza cartons. He reached in and took out a pack of cigarettes, which he pocketed, then stood up and to the side.

A few houses away, Jack and Cameron were visiting Angel. They were hanging out like they always did, smoking cigarettes, Angel doing so despite the fact that she was pregnant. They were talking about scams when they heard a loud pop.

"F---!" Angel exclaimed.

"Was that it?" Jack asked.

"That was it!" Cameron confirmed.

A neat, red hole had materialized in the back of Aaron Iturra's head. Iturra slumped back down, the mattress suddenly turning a dark red. Carrie came awake instantly and screamed, "Help me, somebody come and help me." Elstad and Brown turned and ran. Soon, they were back on the street and Elstad turned to Brown.

"I can't believe it. I shot that muthaf---er in the back of the head," he said with a great big smile.

Not a minute later, the boys came running in the door of the house that Jim shared with his sister Angel and their parents. Shaking violently, Jim Elstad declared, "I did it! I did it!"

Angel looked at her brother and smiled.

"Well, how do you feel?"

All of the Crips in the room looked at Jim, who beamed proudly, like the kid who had sunk the big basket with regulation time gone.

"I feel great! 'Cause you get such a thrill from it, you know?"

"Yeah, you get a real thrill from it," Joe Brown repeated.

Joe opened his fist. There on his palm, for all to see, were four bullets and one spent shell.

"Oh, God," said Angel.

They all looked at her. Water was seeping down her leg.

"My God, it's coming!" she screamed.

"Somebody come and help us! Somebody come and help us!"

Some sound, some feeling, *something* roused Janyce Iturra to consciousness. It was the TV, she thought, that was it. Darn you, Aaron, you left the TV on. He'd been watching TV in the living room and had fallen asleep on the couch. Which happened a lot.

Janyce got up and went into the living room. Her first thought was "Oh, my God, it's dark!" Then, as her sleep-shrouded mind cleared, she heard the plaintive cries again. "Somebody come and help us! Somebody come and help us!"

Janyce's adrenaline began to pump and she could feel her heart pounding in her chest as she ran through the living room and the kitchen into the garage area, to Aaron's room. The door was open a crack and she just bashed right in.

Carrie's mouth froze in fear when she saw her. *I scared the heck out of her*, Janyce thought, seeing the pale, frightened expression on the young girl's face.

"Oh, God, it's you!" said Carrie.

"What?"

"I don't know, I don't know," Carrie muttered. For a moment, Carrie's sad face and eyes looked even sadder, making her seem older than her twenty-two years. Janyce looked over at Aaron and suddenly, everything was blocked out. She heard nothing, saw nothing but the bloody picture in front of her.

Her first-born son lay prone on the bed, a gash on the top of his head, on the upper part of the right eye. *Oh, my God, somebody has bashed Aaron in the head*, Janyce thought.

"Carrie, call 911."

Carrie ran out to the living room where the phone was, just as a commotion began. Janyce's teenage daughter Tina came running into the bedroom.

Seeing her brother, Tina asked anxiously, "What happened?"

"Somebody has bashed Aaron on the head," Janyce answered grimly and looked down. "You're going to be okay, Aaron, you're as strong as they come," she said to the unconscious boy.

Janyce glanced into the living room. Carrie stood motionless at the phone. She had gone into shock and couldn't even dial 911.

"Tina, go get me your phone," Janyce ordered.

Tina's phone had a fifty-foot cord on it. She went back to her bedroom to drag it in. Janyce's eyes trailed Tina down the hallway. Her other three kids were all standing at the back of the hallway screaming, talking, wondering what was happening.

"Tina, get the damn phone!" Janyce shouted over and over until finally, Tina came back with it. "Get me some towels, get me some towels," Janyce screamed.

Though there wasn't a lot of blood on Aaron's face, she wanted to use the towels to put pressure on the head wound.

"Hello, this is 911."

"Yes, I need, ugh, help, an ambulance," Janyce shouted, continuing to apply pressure to the wound. She cradled Aaron in her arms with one hand, while trying to support him with the other. It was a struggle just to keep his 230-pound, six-foot-five body from sagging to the floor.

The 911 operator, working out of Public Safety's Central Lane County Communication Center, listened as Janyce described the head injury, then ordered Janyce to "get him on his back." Aaron was on his side. Janyce's hands were still preoccupied stemming the blood flow, so she used her legs to flip her son over. That's when she saw the wound on the other side of his head. That made two, front and back, where someone smashed his head in, Janyce thought.

"Keep the kids out of here! Keep them out of here!" she screamed at Tina. It was a strange scene, everyone running around wildly like Europeans at a soccer match, Aaron lying on the floor with a serious expression on his unblemished face while a pool of blood formed around his head in a sort of halo that seeped out farther and farther until it reached the vestibule of the doorway. Janyce picked up the phone. The 911 operator was still there.

"Where are you?" the operator asked calmly.

"We're in a panhandle, we're in a panhandle!" she kept repeating into the phone, and then gave the address. "You can't see our house from the street, you know, but the address is out there," Janyce continued, growing hysterical.

Aaron's head lolled to the side and Janyce picked it back up, trying to keep his airway open. Putting her other hand on the wall for balance, she continued to apply pressure to the head wounds. She paused for a second and listened. Thank God he was still breathing.

"What's your address?"

On the other end of the line, Janyce could hear the operator typing into her computer.

"1310 Rutledge Street."

"Okay, an ambulance is on the way."

It seemed like an eternity, but finally, Janyce heard the sounds of sirens approaching. The ambulance pulled into the driveway and she could hear a door being opened, a stretcher being wheeled out and in between, the talk of cops who had arrived on the scene and the static and crackle of their CB radios.

The paramedics pushed Janyce out of the way, and began working on Aaron. Uniformed cops, prompted by the 911 report, flooded into the house. Once he was stabilized, the paramedics loaded Aaron onto the gurney. By then, Carrie was still in the living room in a state of shock, the kids were in the kitchen wondering what was going on and Janyce was ready to hop in the ambulance with Aaron. As she started out with her son, a plainclothes cop, who had recently arrived on the scene, stopped her.

"But I'm going to the hospital with my son," Janyce protested.

"I don't think so," said the cop. "You're not going anywhere."

"What do you mean? That's my son! Somebody bashed him in the head."

The cop looked sad. He looked around and saw the kids. "Why don't you go into the kitchen with your kids?" he suggested in a gentle but firm tone. Somewhat confused, Janyce went into the kitchen, catching the barest of glances as Aaron's ambulance sped off for Sacred Heart Hospital. The ambulance siren receded into the distance.

What the hell am I waiting for? Janyce thought. *Why are they making me wait?*

It seemed to Janyce that she was kept in the kitchen for a long time. There was a cop posted at every door of the house, and two or three were always with her in the kitchen. Sometimes, the cops thought they heard some noise outside, and one of them always went to check it out. Each time they came back and said, "Nothing," sounding disappointed.

What was actually happening, though Janyce didn't know it at the time, was that the cops were securing the crime scene and hoping that whoever had hurt Aaron might be coming back for something they had left. Such things did happen, though rarely.

Janyce looked down at her hands and suddenly discovered that they were covered with Aaron's blood. In all the excitement, she had forgotten about that. She went over to the sink to wash it off. She turned the faucet on, fiddled with the hot and cold water, and was just about to plunge her hands in when one of the cops yelled, "Stop!"

No one, least of all police officers, wanted someone to be killed just so that they could solve the case. But they were prone to boredom just as much as the next guy. A year could go by in law enforcement without anything really interesting happening. Oh, there'd be an occasional homicide, a crime of passion where a husband killed his wife for cheating on him, or vice versa, nothing some rookie couldn't solve, and then *Kaboom!* There'd be a case that tried everything in you and you were right back in it again.

In the Eugene Department of Public Safety, there were four trial teams that worked homicides. Jim Michaud was a trial team leader. In short, that meant that when his number was punched, he had a murder to solve. So when his beeper awoke Michaud out of a sound sleep, the best he could hope for was a case really worth getting out of a warm, comfortable bed for.

He pulled his lanky body up, reached for the beeper,

looked at the number on the LCD, picked up the phone beside the bed and dialed. After a moment, someone answered.

"Michaud here," he said in a flat, nasal twang. Listening, he nodded a few times. Next to him, Paula slept soundly. She had been through this before.

"Yes, I know where it is," he said into the receiver, then hung up.

In the decade prior to the Iturra murder, some believed that the power and ability of the Eugene Police Department to do their jobs had been compromised by a string of city managers who had de-emphasized the department's role in maintaining public safety. Perhaps it was the liberal leanings of the town that had brought the changes on. Whatever it was, cops on the street no longer felt that they had the support of their bosses.

Lately, the Chief had been floating a new plan around. The idea was to take experienced investigators like Michaud and rotate them back to uniform. This way, everybody got a chance to move up the ranks, and seasoned veterans got to go out on the street again. Never mind that inexperienced officers would just muck up a crime scene. Michaud had found that logic had nothing to do with the decisions the brass made.

By the time Michaud arrived at the crime scene in his 1993 Ford Taurus, it was threatening rain. Still, Michaud never wore a rain coat or carried an umbrella. He figured it was bad luck.

Jim Michaud strode through the crowd of cops and medical personnel who were milling around out in front of the house. With his tall, rangy good looks and confident stride, he looked like a professional athlete, instead of what he really was: a senior detective in the Violent Crimes Squad of the Eugene Department of Public Safety.

"Hi, Steve," he said to Steve Skelton, the d.a.'s man.

"Jim," Skelton nodded.

Skelton, an assistant district attorney, was there to provide support if the detectives had any legal questions regarding removal of evidence, interviewing subjects or anything else that might have a legal bearing on the case.

"Hey, Les, what have we got?" Detective Michaud asked his partner Les Rainey.

"A kid was shot. Execution style. One to the head. Looks like a forty-five," said the detective, consulting his notebook. "He's not expected to make it through the night. Mother's in the kitchen. She's pretty upset about the gunpowder test."

Before he went in to talk to the mother, Michaud entered the garage bedroom and looked at the crime scene. There was a pool of blood on the bed where the victim was shot down, with spattering on the walls. A crime-scene photographer stood off to the side taking shots of the room from various angles.

It used to be that the Eugene Police Department sent their crime-scene shots out to local Pacific Photo for developing. Lately, a police lab had been established to do the work, which in Michaud's opinion was unfortunate, because Pacific Photo had done a better job.

"Have you found the bullet?" Michaud asked one of the crime-scene technicians who was examining the blood spatter on the walls.

"Not yet," he muttered.

"Keep looking."

He found Janyce seated in the kitchen. After Michaud introduced himself, she peppered him with questions.

Why did they keep her at the house? Why did they stop her from visiting her son? And why did she have to take that test? Michaud shot a look at the other cops at the scene, who wouldn't meet his gaze.

"Oh, my God, you don't know yet," Michaud muttered.

"What?"

He took her outside to his car and sat her down.

"I'm sorry to have to tell you, but Aaron was shot . . ."

"What are you talking about?" Janyce asked innocently, almost defensively. "He had a gash over his eye."

"Well, I hate to tell you this, but Aaron was shot in the back of the head."

"So what was the wound on top of the head, on the forehead?"

"That's the exit wound. The place where the bullet came out."

"No way. No way. There's no way! You can't tell me that!" Janyce shouted.

"I have to tell you this. We've gotten a report from the hospital and it says he's still alive. But, I don't think there's much of a chance."

"Who would do this? Why would they do this?" Janyce asked, sinking into numb grief.

"We don't know. What happened?"

"Well, I—I was basically sleeping and I didn't hear no gunshot or anything, didn't hear no people or anything. Then I thought I heard the TV, got up, walked through the house and wound up in Aaron's room. You know the rest."

"Do you know anyone who would want your son dead, Mrs. Iturra?"

"No way!" Janyce repeated. "And how come they won't let me wash my hands?"

"We need to test them for gunpowder. It's routine in cases like this. Everyone in a house where a shooting takes place gets their hands tested for gunpowder residue."

"There's no way." Janyce firmly shook her head. "You can test me but you are not gonna do my children. They have nothing to do with this."

At that point, the technician who was going to administer the gunpowder tests arrived. After a briefing by Michaud, she began testing Janyce and her kids. As ridiculous as the thought of her or her kids shooting Aaron was, Janyce knew no point would be gained by arguing with the cops. Best to take the test and get it over with. When no trace of gunpowder showed up on her hands, Janyce felt momentarily smug.

"See, I told you," she said.

"It's just procedure," Michaud answered sympathetically.

"Now please let me go to the hospital," Janyce continued, looking at the kitchen clock that said 4 a.m.

"Best to wait until the representative from Victims Services arrives," said Michaud.

Victims Services is a relatively new type of agency in law enforcement departments nationwide. They function as compassionate advocates for victims and their families, simultaneously helping them negotiate the treacherous waters of grief on one shore and the court system on the other.

Michaud didn't want to take any chance that Janyce wasn't telling the whole truth, that she might really know who had killed her son and go after them. He doubted it, but in his line of work, you learned that anyone was capable of murder with the right kind of provocation. Best to play this situation by the book.

At the same moment Jim Michaud was telling Janyce Iturra the grim news, Joe Brown stood at a secluded spot outside of Eugene on the banks of the Willamette River. Behind him was a station wagon, with its headlights on, illuminating the river. In front of him was raging white water, flashing in a quick torrent over rocks in the river bed. To his right, in the encroaching darkness, he just barely made out the dark forms of trees that lined the banks. To his left was a little island that had formed in the river where the water table had gotten too low. It was a perfect place for concealment. Dark, silent, alone.

Brown reached in his pocket and came out with the crumpled pack of cigarettes he had taken from the girl's pocketbook. He shook one out and lit it, savoring the smoke going into his lungs, calming him down. Then quickly, he emptied the revolver of the remaining five bullets. Reeling back his arm, he threw them out as far as he could. He didn't make the rapids.

The bullets sailed out into the water about fifty feet from the bank and fell into shallow water. Still, that was okay; the river bottom was brown. They'd just blend in. So would the gun, which he tossed in a moment later. It sank rapidly into the silt.

There. Over and done with like nothing had happened.

Joe Brown turned sharply and walked back to the car. He got in and closed the door. The wagon backed up and turned onto a ribbon of concrete that paralleled the river. They drove for a while, then turned down a side street, stopping to rest in front of Brown's home. He got out, then leaned back in the open window and said to the driver, "See you tomorrow, Moms."

The woman he had called "Moms" watched as he ran up the driveway and disappeared inside.

Lisa Fentress awakened from her marijuana-induced sleep to the sound of her phone ringing.

Who was that? she wondered.

She couldn't be sure, and she didn't care. She liked where she was, half asleep and half awake. Didn't have to deal with anything. Didn't have to see anyone. Didn't have to have any responsibility for what she'd done. Maybe, if she tried, she could make the phone go away.

After a while, the phone stopped ringing and Lisa floated back into cannabis dreams.

At 5 a.m., Lisa awoke when her pager went off. She dialed the number on the digital display.

"Aaron was taken care of," said the voice on the other end of the line.

THREE

AT 7 A.M., HEATHER Parr, the woman from Victims Services, finally showed up. She had come from home, where she left her sleeping daughter.

As angry as Janyce was that they had to wait, she had to admit that Aaron's shooting had so shaken her up, she didn't know if she would have had the wherewithal to drive herself and the kids to the hospital.

"Come on," said Parr, and Janyce and the kids piled into a van that Victims Services had provided. Parr, ever obliging, drove quickly to the hospital.

Once there, they ran quickly through an emergency room gauntlet of overworked doctors and nurses and orderlies. They found Aaron upstairs in the Intensive Care Unit. Standing off in the shadows was a uniformed police officer, whom Michaud had placed there as a guard.

"We can only allow you to go in one at a time," said the unit's head nurse. Janyce went in first, putting on a gown and washing her hands to make sure she didn't track in any germs.

She found Aaron attached to a respirator, heart monitor and IV tubes. Looking down at her son, he seemed so small and helpless. *You're still my baby*, she thought, gazing at his face, pristine and rested despite his serious injury.

"Who did this to my baby?" she asked aloud.

Suddenly, there was another person standing at her side. It was the head nurse again.

"Mrs. Iturra, I'm sorry to bother you, but has anyone told you about your son's condition? Do you understand the extent of your son's injuries?"

Janyce felt relieved. Finally, someone to tell her the truth, here and now, with none of this waiting.

"No, I don't know what's going on with him. Tell me."

"Well, the bullet went in the left side of his head and exited out of the right. In the process, it did a lot of damage inside. There is very little, or no brain activity."

"But he's still alive!"

"Yes, but—"

"His heart is still pumping, he's breathing, he's a very, very strong kid."

"I understand, Mrs. Iturra, but frankly, it's not going to be long before his heart stops."

Despite what she wanted to believe, Janyce could tell that the woman was telling the truth. "My kids need to say goodbye." The nurse nodded.

As Janyce watched, the kids came in, one at a time. She didn't have the heart to tell them that he was going to die. She just couldn't do that to them. But they knew, the way people always know when placed in such an awful situation. Finally, when she was alone again with Aaron, she leaned over the bed and reached out to hug her first-born.

"I can't let you do that," said the cop, who got out of his chair.

"But . . ."

"Ma'am, I'm sorry."

"Well, could I just hold his hand?"

"Sure."

Janyce picked up Aaron's hand and held it to her cheek, where it brushed against her tears. She reached out and touched her fingertips to his chest, remembering feeding him as a child, the way he squirmed in her arms when she gave him the bottle, and the way he looked up at her with that broad, easy smile, happy to see her. Always. And what made it worse, what *really* made it worse, was that he was her best friend.

Janyce had separated from her husband, Aaron's stepfather, just weeks before, and while she had seen it coming, the impact was no less great. One moment he was there and the next moment he wasn't.

After that, she had leaned on Aaron. The kid was always there for her. Now, who could she lean on?

When, in 1977, twenty-two-year-old Janyce Iturra got pregnant with Aaron it was not a good situation.

Many of the Indians of the northwest tribes that Lewis and Clark had communed with in 1805 had been wiped out by government genocide. Three of the indigenous tribes had since banded together, signed a treaty with the government and lived on Oregon's Warm Springs Reservation. Aaron Iturra's father was one of those Indians.

After his brief affair with Janyce, she had gotten pregnant. It was not a planned pregnancy and yet, she had no desire to abort. She traveled to Bethel, a suburb of Seattle, where she gave birth.

Up until Aaron's birth, Janyce had been a child of the streets. She had always been a good person, but she drank too much and just didn't care about anyone or anything, including herself. Pregnancy and childbirth made her a responsible adult. In return, she made Aaron a guarantee. "As long as we're together, we're gonna make it through this life," she promised the baby in her arms. "I'm gonna do my very best to make life the best for you."

Despite the drawbacks she faced in the intervening years, whether it was dead-end jobs or dead-end relationships, she always thought, "Thank God I got pregnant. Thank God I got you."

And Aaron was always there for her.

"Mom, you can do this. We'll make it. We'll make it," Aaron encouraged her time and time again.

She had been a single parent living on just her income for support. She wouldn't even let her kids work to help with the bills. Her goals, first and foremost, were for her kids to get a good education, without which she knew they would never get anywhere. Janyce herself had gone through three years at Portland State University, but had never finished. She had not graduated from college, but she wanted them to.

As late as a few weeks before the shooting, when Aaron's stepdad, the only father he ever really knew, left the family, Aaron was still encouraging Janyce, assuring her that things would work out for the better. And now, with him dying, Janyce felt she was reneging on her half of their bargain. She had not kept him safe and she could not save his life. Someone had come along to steal it. A thief in the night with a long, smoking gun.

By 10:30 a.m., all signs of brain activity had ceased. The nurse came up to Janyce.

"Ma'am I know this is a bad time. But I need to ask you a question."

"Which is?"

"Do you think your son would have been willing to donate his organs?"

There wasn't even any anger. Janyce knew her son was dead. Only the respirator was keeping his heart going. She summoned Tina. Together, they went down the hallway and stood off to the side, in the same spot many people before them had stood, having to make the same type of difficult choice. Unlike the movies, questions of when to turn a respirator off, when to use extraordinary life-saving methods on a terminal patient, or whether organs should be donated for transplant are not made in bright doctors' offices, or spanking-new suburban homes. Those decisions are made in dim, puke-painted hospital corridors, like the one Tina and Janyce found themselves in now.

"What do you think, Tina?" Janyce asked.

"Mom, there's no choice. You know how Aaron feels about that."

Aaron had actually been prescient enough to have discussed the possibility of what to do with his organs if he died before his time. And now that time was here.

"That's what I would like," Aaron had said. "If I saved just one other life, maybe my death would be worth it."

"Okay," Janyce answered.

She had known what she was going to do before she took the walk with Tina. She just wanted support for that decision. "I'll sign the papers," Janyce told the nurse. After signing, Janyce walked back into the hospital room. She leaned down and kissed Aaron on the forehead.

"I love you, Aaron."

Her reply was a sudden ringing noise as the EKG flatlined and Aaron died peacefully. Janyce and the children left. Then, the medical staff went to work.

Aaron's body was rushed upstairs to the operating room where a surgical team was waiting. Standing to the side were five white-robed messengers of life, each carrying a single Igloo cooler well-stocked with ice. This was not "Touched by an Angel."

When they left a short while later, each cooler held a precious cargo: Aaron's heart, kidneys, pancreas and liver. Janyce would later write to Tom Jacobsen, the fifty-year-old Baptist minister who received Aaron's heart, and the four others whose lives were saved by Aaron's organs.

Some might consider it a fair trade—one life for five. But to Jim Michaud it was murder plain and simple.

Michaud had heard from the officer on duty at the hospital about Aaron's death. That made this a murder investigation now. Time to put it into high gear.

Michaud arrived at the police morgue just as the forensic pathologist was making the "Y" incision on Aaron's chest for the autopsy. Quickly, he changed into blue scrubs. A police photographer was already there taking pictures of the proceedings. While that was being done, Michaud called the crime lab.

"Any luck finding the bullet?"

"We stripped his room. Took everything out of it, peeled the carpet out. Even took a wall apart," said a crime-scene technician.

"And you're telling me you found nothing?"

"Nothing," the technician echoed. Which meant everything from this point onward about the murder weapon was guesswork.

There's a ton of cops that will tell you, Michaud thought, *what is an entrance and exit wound just by eyeballing the body*. But it was only by examining the body under the forensic pathologist's knife that the investigator could accurately figure out the kind of bullets, the distance from which they were fired, the forensic evidence that could eventually be used to convict the killer.

The forensic pathologist conducting the autopsy used an electric saw to take off the skull cap and peer into Aaron's brain. Michaud noticed chipping on the inside, in the back of Aaron's skull, indicating the entrance wound. Over his forehead, on the side, he saw the bone chips on the outside, indicating the exit wound.

"Any sign of the bullet, doc?"

The pathologist shook his head.

It must have fallen out when the paramedics picked him up, or on the way to the ambulance. *Kind of like the J.F.K. bullet*, Michaud thought, that had gone through the President's neck and Governor John Connally's shoulder and wrist, finally coming to rest in Connally's thigh. Having lost eighty per cent of its velocity, it was just able to penetrate the skin.

While many discounted that scenario, Michaud knew from his experience with firearms and bullet wounds that the skull could easily slow a bullet to the point where, when it exited, it had little or no velocity and literally just fell to the ground. He would instruct the technicians to comb the crime scene again.

Soon, they were fitting the skull cap back on, and examining the entrance wound more closely, figuring out the trajectory of the bullet.

"He was shot lying down, wasn't he?" Michaud asked the forensic pathologist.

"Looks like it," the pathologist replied.

Probably from about six feet away, Michaud figured, from the look of the wound. *And there's no speckling or any powder burns here or tattooing from unburnt powder.* Yes, definitely far enough away to get off a good shot, but not too far to hinder accuracy.

Whoever did this was able to sneak cold-bloodedly into the Iturra home and commit this execution while Aaron and his girlfriend slept. *Someone is filling a contract*, Michaud thought. This was a *hit*, a murder that someone contracted for.

"Turn him," Michaud ordered the police photographer.

Together they turned Aaron's body over. In anticipation of the killer's capture and the subsequent trial, the preparation of exhibits starts in the coroner's bleak, antiseptic examining room.

With Aaron on his stomach, just as he was when he was shot, the photographer took a photograph of him from the same angle the killer would have been standing when he fired the deadly shot. In this way, some future jury could actually picture the way the crime occurred.

An hour later, Michaud was home. Paula had already left for work. He figured to take a shower, get into some new clothes and then head back to the office.

Michaud put on a freshly starched white shirt, admiring how clean it smelled. And then he flashed back to the coroner's autopsy room and smelled Aaron's body, a combination of odors, of urine and feces released at the time of death, and flesh beginning to putrefy. Cops are good at putting that wall up between their professional and home lives but seeing such a young man murdered in cold blood, it was the kind of thing you know you're never going to forget.

Michaud thanked his lucky stars that Aaron had not been a fire victim. They've got that sweet smell to them that drove him nuts.

FOUR

DEATH IS BAD ENOUGH, especially when·it happens to a teenager with everything to live for. It is worse when the deceased is the victim of a violent crime and his family cannot go back home because home is still considered a crime scene.

Janyce and the kids went back to the house, where technicians were still processing evidence. The family picked up some clothes and went to Janyce's friend Diana's house to stay the night, until the police would let them go home.

When they got to Diana's at 12:30, the first thing Janyce did was call Mary Thompson. She needed to let her know what had happened. She didn't want Mary to hear the news on TV.

Janyce went through her purse for Mary's number and found it. Janyce dialed, got her phone answering machine and left a message with Diana's number. She expected to get a call back quickly. Minutes stretched into hours without a response.

Over the course of the day, Janyce tried Mary fifteen times. She was looking for support from another adult. She had her kids, of course, and Diana, but it wasn't enough. She needed Mary, who'd been through tragedy with her son Beau. All she wanted was to hear her voice; Janyce needed to let her know. She dialed, and dialed, and dialed. Each time, she got a message and left her number. Each time, there was no return call.

I guess I'll see her at Aaron's funeral. She'll be there. She's our friend. She cared for Aaron, Janyce thought. It was this commitment, to friends and family and her cause, that first impressed Janyce Iturra when Mary called her house a year before.

"Hi, I'd like to speak to Aaron Iturra," said a female voice.

"Who's this?" Janyce Iturra had asked.

"Mary Thompson," answered the voice. "I—"

"Oh, we just saw you on TV."

"Well, I guess maybe they exaggerated just a little," Mary said modestly.

"I don't think so," said Janyce. "You have quite a message there."

The media had started picking up on Mary's anti-gang crusade. The local newspaper, *The Register Guard*, featured her in a front-page story about Eugene's gangs. In it, Chuck Tilby, a senior member of the Eugene Department of Public Safety's anti-gang task force said, "I wish we had a hundred of her. She's opened her eyes and realizes that there's a huge draw out there for kids to gangs and that it's leading to criminal behavior.

"She's willing to get involved to try to change that. It's interesting to find a crusader who seems to be able to keep things in perspective, who can connect with these kids without going into a Chicken Little posture."

The article went on to describe Thompson this way: "To youth gang members, the 39-year-old Thompson is a den mother of sorts. She knows their real names and their street tags. She knows where they hang out and what their graffiti spells. She can flash [gang] hand signals and run off phrases of cryptic slang as quickly as any 14-year-old [gang member]."

"I try to fight back against gangs, but I also try to understand the gang issues," Mary is quoted in the article. "They're people too and they're doing this for a reason. I figure if I can get close to the source I'll be able to understand it a little better."

Cautioning adults, she concluded, "Parents need to know who their kids are hanging out with, what's in their notebooks, what's in their pockets. And they need to know where they are at 2 a.m.

"I knew where Beau was all my waking hours, but I didn't know 'Bishop' the gang member was crawling out his bedroom window at 2 every morning."

It was an impressive story, and television and radio stations dispatched reporters to record her when she counseled kids against joining gangs. Camera crews followed Mary down the street as she pointed out gang graffiti. Mary was opening parents' eyes to this growing menace.

On television, there didn't seem to be anything special about her at first. Just under forty, Mary Thompson was tall and stocky, with short, reddish-brown hair. She really looked ordinary, until the camera caught her eyes. They were intense, drawing you in with the fervor behind her words. Charismatic.

"Well, I'm going into schools to counsel against joining gangs, and I'm looking for kids other kids listen to, to join me," Mary told Janyce during their first conversation. "And I understand that Aaron is exactly the type of kid I should have on our side."

"Oh, Aaron is violently against gangs," Janyce answered. "And I know he'd love to join you."

She was right; Aaron liked to help people and what better way than to help them avoid the gang lifestyle that never led anyone anywhere but to prison or an early grave? Aaron Iturra readily joined Mary's anti-gang crusade.

Mary stopped by the Iturra house frequently to take Aaron with her to gang-prevention seminars. While waiting for Aaron to get ready, Mary and Janyce would talk. They had so much in common.

"Beau's my life, Beau's my life. I would do anything to protect Beau," Mary told Janyce.

"I understand that," Janyce, an attractive, middle-aged woman, answered. "Aaron is my life too. He's our rock. I hardly ever lock my doors. My son is our protector. His four brothers and sisters idolize him." It was then that Aaron appeared.

Aaron had the striking features of his Indian ancestors. At six-foot-five and 230 pounds, he was the kind of person people looked up to, literally and figuratively. Though he had had some skirmishes with gangs, Aaron had rejected them and remained proudly independent. No one messed with him.

During subsequent conversations, Mary asked Aaron to keep Beau out of trouble. She wanted the older boy to assume the role of protector for the younger. Aaron agreed, but no matter how much Janyce and Mary wanted to keep their kids from turning to the dark side, over the next few years, Eugene's growing gang community continued to seduce its young.

* * *

Jim Michaud drove his car into the underground garage that housed the department's unmarked police vehicles. After getting out, he happened to glance at his new set of license plates. They said "40202." A twenty-two-year veteran of the force, the numbers stood for his retirement date—April 2, 2002.

When the city manager of Eugene publicly declared that cops should stop talking so much about their retirement dates, Detective Jim Michaud promptly went out and got his new plate. That was Michaud: always bucking authority. And his superiors stood for it because Michaud was the best investigator in the Violent Crimes Squad. Never mind that he was the department's union negotiator, who beat their butts come contract time. The bottom line was, he cleared cases.

Michaud walked up the stairs into a low-lying, official-looking white building. This was the Department of Public Safety, one of a series of such buildings located in downtown Eugene. The Violent Crimes Squad occupied a small run-down office on the first floor. The squad room was long and narrow, filled with ten sets of hand-me-down furniture that lined the perimeter of the room.

On Michaud's desk, in the far corner on the left, were three piles of folders. Each represented cases that he characterized as: "front burner," "back burner" and "double-wrapped freezer."

The double-wrapped freezer pile consisted of cases that had grown as cold as a corpse in the morgue; the back burner cases would get solved eventually; the front burner cases were hot and had to be solved now. At the top of his front burner pile was the Iturra case.

Iturra's gang connection seemed the logical place to

start. Eugene had two officers who specialized in gang activity and intelligence. One of them was Detective Ric Raynor, the other Chuck Tilby. Michaud called Raynor. After exchanging pleasantries, Raynor volunteered that he had a great contact in the gang community.

"Who's that?" Michaud asked.

"Mary Thompson. The papers call her 'Gang Mom.' "

"Yeah, I saw her on some TV report a while back."

It had been the same news segment Janyce Iturra had seen, with Mary showing gang graffiti on camera. The difference was, Mary had looked familiar to Michaud. He had seen her someplace before. But he'd soon forgotten about her after the segment aired. Maybe in his files . . .

"Mary's very influential in the gang community," Raynor continued. "Mary can talk gang talk and gang slang as good as any gangster on the street. She could convince somebody to turn themselves in to me. I'll go out and talk to her immediately."

"Thanks, Ric," Michaud said, and hung up. He turned to his filing cabinet and began rifling through it.

Mary Thompson had first come to see Ric Raynor in early 1994. She was concerned about Beau's involvement with gangs and didn't know what to do about it. Raynor was immediately impressed by her concern, her intelligence, her willingness to do something about what was happening to her son and the city's youth, who were getting sucked up into the gang lifestyle.

In order to combat gangs, Raynor felt, you needed to understand them. At first, Mary was totally ignorant. But over time, she came to develop a working knowledge of gangs on the street. Raynor and others in the police department felt that she came by her knowledge the hard way, by monitoring her son's street activities.

Mary had also become an advocate for kids, showing them that she understood the pressures they were under, the lack of love in their home lives and the lure of the gangs, which provided a sense of family and empowerment at the same time.

Raynor was impressed with the way that, over the next few years, Mary had learned the intricacies of the gang lifestyle. She knew what wearing gang rags or colors meant, what secret signs gangs used to communicate with one another, and what *sets*, gang subdivisions, were.

Mary could talk the talk and walk the walk as well as any gang member. She was "cool," respected by gangsters and cops alike for her impartiality, her sensitivity, her compassion. What was most impressive was her influence with the gangs.

As Raynor told Michaud, Mary could convince a kid involved with a crime to turn himself into the cops or, for that matter, she could influence him to talk or not talk to the cops, to associate or not associate with a particular gang cop. In short, she had power on both sides, in the criminal gang community and in law enforcement. She was a modern-day power broker among the disenfranchised young people of the city of Eugene.

Raynor drove out from downtown Eugene to interview Thompson. He felt certain that her network of teenage gang members would tell her what had happened.

Mary Thompson worked as a security guard for a local department store, but because she worked a later shift, she was home when Raynor drove up.

"Hi, Ric," she said when she answered the door of her home.

"Mary," Raynor said, and nodded at the stocky woman with the large eyes behind the owlish glasses.

Ric Raynor liked and respected Mary Thompson. He often phoned her when he was out looking for teenage suspects. She, in turn, paged him all the time with information on gang activities. He thought of her as a concerned mother who had gotten involved in her anti-gang activity to alert the community to a pressing social problem.

"Mary, Aaron Iturra's been murdered."

"I heard. It's been on the news." She looked down in grief. "I really liked Aaron."

"I know you did, Mary. Can you think of anyone who had it in for him, anyone who'd want him dead?"

She hesitated. Raynor knew she didn't want to be thought of as a *stoolie*. Her effectiveness as an anti-gang activist depended on the goodwill and respect she had built up among the city's gang population. She didn't want to blow that by becoming an informer. But at the same time, Aaron was a boy whom she had liked a lot.

"Okay, look," she began. "There was this guy who came around to see me."

"When?"

"Around a week ago."

"Driving?"

"Yeah, a black Acura. Said he was a gang member up in Portland. He said his name was Sonny and sat on my couch and wanted to know about this thing at the Grocery Cart and wanted to know about Aaron. And, I wouldn't tell him very much about Aaron because he wanted a picture. And, he wanted me to tell him where he lived and I wouldn't tell him that."

"Tell him anything?"

Mary hesitated.

"Sonny, he was a scary-looking dude. I was afraid if I didn't tell him something, he'd come back again and this time he'd be looking for me."

"So what did you tell him?"

"The truth. That Aaron was released from jail with no charges and that he lied in the police report."

"Then what happened?"

Mary shrugged. "He left." She gave Raynor a description of Sonny. Other than that, she didn't know anything else. But she did have a question.

"Ric, isn't there some kind of test you guys do when you think someone's fired a gun?"

"Yeah, a paraffin test. Why?"

"And the idea is to determine if someone fired a gun recently, right?"

"Right. So why you asking all this?"

"Because I'm thinking that maybe that's a way for you guys to get to the bottom of this. If you can get this guy Sonny and give him the test and it confirms that he fired a gun, then you'd have your shooter."

"Exactly. But we have to find him first."

"Know what kind of caliber the bullet was?"

"Not yet."

It was a highly unusual exchange. Unlike "The Rockford Files," for example, cops didn't regularly release information on an active investigation to a civilian, but Mary Thompson wasn't just some ordinary person.

Back at headquarters a short time later, Raynor told Michaud of his conversation with "Gang Mom." Michaud thanked him for his help and proceeded to make some inquiries of Portland police. After interviewing them, and conducting an exhaustive search of computer records, no gang member named "Sonny" was found in the Portland area, or any place else in Oregon. Michaud called Raynor back into his office.

"I think Mary's lying. I think she's heavily involved," Michaud told Raynor.

Raynor, though, preferred to believe her involvement was more peripheral. Maybe she knew who the shooters were and just wasn't telling out of fear she'd lose the respect of the gang members she regularly counseled.

After Raynor went back to his office, Michaud felt uneasy. He was afraid that Raynor's close contact with Thompson might be clouding his judgment. Michaud turned back to his desk and plucked a folder from the "hot" pile that he had unearthed earlier from his files. It contained the record of his first contact with Mary Thompson. Only at that time, her name wasn't Thompson.

It was Fockler.

TWO

The Investigation

FIVE

WHEN MARY FOCKLER LEFT Cleveland in early 1978, she hitchhiked to Oregon. Almost immediately, her life began to change radically.

Mary was pregnant. She wasn't sure who the father was, but she suspected it was a fellow Cleveland native she had had a brief fling with before she moved west. Regardless, she now had a baby on the way and no visible means of support.

Mary settled in the funky rural community of Wolf Creek, Oregon. Maybe she was looking for a father figure; it is hard to tell. What is clear is that she met *Frank Wilman*, a man thirty-one years her senior. They hit it off and decided to live together. Wilman was apparently not very good with math because when Mary's son Beau was born on August 6, 1978, she told him that Beau was his. Wilman apparently bought this, but Mary decided to give the infant the surname of "Flynn," the boy's probable biological father.

Wilman remembers Beau as being a "good kid." He helped the boy enjoy outdoor sports like horseback riding and fishing. The three had settled into a life together and in 1981, they made it official when Mary and Frank were married. As befits the naturalistic leanings of the community they lived in, the ceremony took place on horseback!

It didn't take long for Mary to get involved in the local drug trade. She would later describe her involvement as being a "field investigator" for the Josephine County Police Department. What she really was was a *snitch*, an informant for money.

Mary made methamphetamines, and she informed on her associates in the drug trade, enough times to accrue a balance of $1100 in her bank account, which she used to beat a hasty retreat from Wolf Creek and its lawbreaking population. She left Beau behind with Frank Wilman.

Starting anew, for a second time, was a priority, but Mary soon realized that leaving her baby behind was no solution to her problems. She came back to Wilman's trailer, where he was living with Beau. She was accompanied by her new boyfriend "Tag." Wilman takes up the story:

"She had ahold of the boy and I had ahold of the boy and I reached up to get my pistol. I pointed it at the floor and I told her that if Tag came in, I'd kill him," Wilman remembers.

Mary eventually got custody and she, Beau and Tag went south to California, stayed a few months and, finding it wasn't the promised land they had hoped for, returned to Wolf Creek. Wilman knew they were back when one day, while he was hanging in his truck outside the post office, Beau came running up.

"Daddy, can we come back?" Beau asked plaintively.

Being a nice guy, Wilman immediately answered "Yes," and Mary and Beau came back to live with him. The reconciliation lasted all of about two weeks. Mary "had a real good personality when she wanted to show it," Wilman recalls, "but she could be ornery too."

As for her friends in Wolf Creek, the ones who had gone to jail because she had snitched on them wanted her dead or worse, while others found they disliked her for her slovenly home. Some even accused her of emotionally and physically abusing Beau. One woman she had snitched on, *Caroline Johnson*, claimed that Mary kept Beau isolated in the back of her home in a separate trailer because she disliked him so. Wilman has a different recollection.

"I guess she was all right as a mother, but there were times when she'd fly off the handle and backhand him for no good reason," says Wilman.

By the spring of 1988, Wilman had once again faded out of the picture, and Mary had become heavily involved in the drug-making business. Methamphetamine had become the drug of choice and Mary knew how to make the stuff and did, but she managed to piss off some of her business associates to the point that once again, she turned to the authorities, this time Detective Dave Claar.

"She said she wanted to get everybody out there busted to keep various people from killing each other," Claar recalls. "She was afraid of something, but I never got the complete story as to why." Regardless of her reason for becoming a snitch again, "She was in the upper echelon of the criminal community when she came to us, so her information was very valuable."

Cops, though, do not like relying on drug users for information, and at the time, Mary was on drugs. The cops made her get clean during the time they worked together so that her information would not be the result of some drug-induced stupor but rather hard information that she meticulously developed.

Claar subsequently found Mary to be "... honest and straightforward." Like many before and since, he also found her to be likable and personable. "She also knows how to play the system and make it work for her," he added.

In return for working with Claar, the detective paid for the relocation of Mary, Beau and her new boyfriend and future husband John Thompson to the Eugene area. "I got letters [from Mary] thanking me for saving her life," Claar says.

Mary was appreciative of the break Claar had given her, an opportunity to start life anew. Not wishing to blow it this time, she married John Thompson in 1992 and took a job as a secretary at a sign-making company outside Eugene. She also took his last name, and thereafter, on all official documents, she used her married name. But people still called her "Mary."

A few months after Mary went to work at the sign maker's, *Bryan Alper*, the owner, discovered that he was mysteriously losing money. A comparison between debits and accounts receivable showed that things didn't match. Cash was finding its way out of the business. Alper had never had any experience with employee embezzlement but, as much as he hated to admit it, that's what seemed to be happening. Any number of people had access to the cash that came in. He knew that he didn't have the expertise to figure out who was taking it, but he had a good buddy who did.

"Hi, Jim, it's Bryan."

"Hey, Bryan, how's it going?"

"Pretty good. Listen, I think I have an employee embezzlement problem going on."

"You sure? Sure it's not something else?"

Alper gripped the phone harder and thought for a second.

"Nope. I'm sure. You know how meticulous I am."

Jim Michaud sighed.

"Look, would you—"

"Sure, no problem," and Michaud drove out to see his old friend.

After examining the books, Michaud realized that Alper had cause for concern. Someone was ripping him off. The totals just didn't tally.

Systematically, Michaud began looking over employee records, searching for anyone who might be an ex-convict, anyone who might have had a grudge against Alper. He looked through a back file of résumés of present employees. While examining Mary Thompson's, a few things began to call attention to themselves.

It said that she had a BA in biology with a math minor from Kent State University in Ohio. It also said that she had subsequently attended Trent College, a local business school, and completed a six-month course in bookkeeping.

That made absolutely no sense. Why would an educated woman with a math minor need a six-month course in bookkeeping? Then there was the matter of her experience as a police officer. Thompson listed a stint as "Field Investigator" for the Josephine County Police Department. Josephine County was near Eugene. Michaud made some calls and then had a little talk with Mary.

When Mary Thompson came into a private office at Alper's sign business to talk to Michaud, what the detective saw was a stout woman, five-foot-eight, over 160 pounds.

"I talked to a Detective Claar in Josephine County. He says you weren't a field investigator. What you were was a paid drug informant, and you were heavily involved in the drug trade. You also went by the name of 'Fockler,'" said Michaud.

"He's lying," Mary assured him.

"No doubt, no doubt."

"You're just putting me on."

"No I'm not. I'm sure there's no doubt in your mind that what you did qualified as field investigation."

Mary wasn't sure how to take that, which was exactly the way the comment was designed, to get her off-balance.

"And what about Kent State?"

"What about it?"

"Great school?"

She nodded. Michaud looked down at the résumé.

"It says here that you matriculated there."

"Yes I did," she answered assertively.

"Problem is, Mary, I called Kent State. There's no record of your having attended the school."

"Kent State's lying."

"So let's see if I get it. Kent State's lying and Detective Claar's lying."

"Right," said Mary, nodding her head.

"Put yourself in my shoes, Mary," said Michaud gently. "Why should I believe you didn't embezzle the money when you've lied about everything else?"

"Well . . ." and Mary went off into repeated denials, until finally, she admitted that she might have been responsible for some of the money disappearing.

"Well, what do you want to do, Bryan?" Michaud asked Alper after Mary had gone back to her desk.

"If I press charges, there'll be a trial and the whole deal?"

Michaud nodded.

"Well, it might be a little easier just to fire her."

Which he did. And Michaud went back to Eugene and forgot about the case. A few years later, Mary showed up in Eugene as an anti-gang activist. And the legend of "Gang Mom" was born.

As the detective in charge of the case, it was Michaud's job to supervise the detectives in his squad in order to put the case together.

Over the next couple of days, Mary began to have second thoughts about her conversation with Raynor. Michaud, meanwhile, was sending out detectives to interview Angel Elstad, Wayde Hudson, Lisa Fentress, *Larry Martin* and all the other members of the 74 Hoover Crips. Maybe it was just self-serving bull, or maybe it was just a minor act of conscience, but two names that kept coming up in almost every interview were "Crazy" Joe Brown and Jim Elstad. The gang members felt that they were involved in the shootings.

On Thursday, October 6, 1994, before Michaud had a chance to act, Ric Raynor came out of a meeting at City Hall. In the square, waiting to meet him, was Mary Thompson.

"I've got information on Aaron," she said, sounding more than a little emotional.

"Like what?"

"Angel told me that Jim and Joe were involved."

Silence. Raynor stared at her.

"You know more about this. Did Jim tell you?"

"You know I can't tell you. You know what I mean."

Raynor knew that was "gangspeak" for "Yes."

Figuring it was time to get Michaud and Rainey involved, he took Mary to an upstairs interrogation room and, while a detective stayed with her, he went into the Violent Crime Unit to tell the detectives she was there.

"She knows me," Michaud said simply.

"How—" Raynor began, but was interrupted by Michaud's raised hand.

"That's not important now. What is important is for Les and you to do the interview. I'd just antagonize her."

Raynor nodded.

"Okay," said Rainey, "let's do it."

Mary was shown to the "hard" interrogation room. Unlike the soft one, which was painted in soft colors, with comfortable chairs and muted lighting, the room Mary Thompson found herself in looked more like a stockroom. There were boxes piled high on shelves and a big, scarred wooden desk in the center of the room with straight-backed chairs arrayed around it.

"Why don't you sit over there, Mary?" Rainey said politely, offering her a chair that backed up against the wall. Rainey sat down opposite her, and Raynor next to him. On the desk were a pad, pencils and pens and a tape recorder. Rainey reached forward and depressed the "record" button.

SIX

ANYBODY WHO HAS EVER watched "NYPD Blue" knows the routine: get the suspect in an interrogation room, advise them of their Constitutional rights to an attorney during questioning, convince them they don't need one, and then, if they don't confess voluntarily, intimidate them physically to confess. If that doesn't work, beat it out of them.

Uh-uh. Nope. Nada. Hands off.

If every cop working today did it the way "Sipowicz" and "Simone" did it, they'd not only lose their badges immediately, their cases would always be overturned on appeal.

Since the Miranda/Escobedo Supreme Court rulings of the 1960's, suspects are advised of their rights to remain silent and to have a lawyer present both when they are arrested and when they are interrogated.

In Mary's case, she had come in voluntarily to speak with Raynor. She was giving a "statement," not a confession. But the cops couldn't take a chance that she might actually save them time and money and confess, so, on the off-chance that she slipped, which both cops knew was the same chance of say, the Chicago Cubs winning the World Series next year, they had to read her her rights anyway. They did it nice and easy, like reciting poetry. No reason to spook her. Then Rainey began with this gambit:

"Now I know a primary concern for you was that you were not gonna be arrested today and that, in fact, you were going to be allowed to leave. Is that correct?"

"That is a concern, but my first primary concern was safety for my son Beau," Mary answered like any concerned parent.

"Now, you've assured us, Mary, that you did not commit the killing yourself, nor did you do anything with the intent of having someone commit the killing. That correct?"

Rainey didn't believe or disbelieve. He was just repeating what she had said when she denied having participated in Aaron's death.

"Yes, absolutely."

"And I've assured you that if, in fact, that's truthful, although you may be responsible for some other crime, that I don't, certainly, anticipate you being charged for the murder of Aaron Iturra. All right?"

"Right."

A pleasant understanding. Of course, what was really being said was this:

Rainey: "If you lie to me, Mary, your number is up!"

Mary: "I understand that, you moron. You think I'm stupid enough to confess to anything?"

And every cop in his heart of hearts believes that the answer to that question is "Yes!" for one simple reason: *I'm smarter than she is. If she was so smart, she'd be in my seat and I'd be in hers.*

"So based on that, assuming that that's a truthful statement by you, please go ahead and just start from the beginning. What do you know about Aaron's murder?"

Mary took a deep breath.

"Starting from the beginning about what I know about Aaron's death and murder. A lot of crap happened about three weeks ago on the sixteenth of September when my son, Beau Flynn, and Aaron Iturra were arrested at Willamette High School. I was very, very mad and very, very upset."

Rainey raised his eyebrows quizzically. Hell, it worked for "Mr. Spock."

"Aaron had told the police some things that didn't happen," Mary asserted. "And that was indicated to me by the police that were doing the questioning of both kids. And I went home and when all the kids started hearing about it of course they fled to my house because that's what always happens.

"They saw how upset I was over Aaron, over Beau getting arrested and Aaron, you know, just not telling the truth about the incident at the Grocery Cart. And then Aaron was released from jail on the following Monday and he called me for a ride."

Mary could hardly hide the incredulity in her voice. *The nerve of the kid*, Rainey thought, *calling his best friend for a ride*. But this whole thing about the Grocery Cart. What was she talking about?

Like most towns, Eugene had its own particular version of 7-Eleven. In Eugene, these convenience stores went under the name "Grocery Cart." Scattered around the city, they provided two things: a convenient place to pick up stuff at inconvenient hours, and a place for kids to hang out. The 74 Hoover Crips had taken to hanging out at one. And unlike shows such as *Hill Street Blues* that advanced a logical reason for gang members to fight—e.g., over turf—in real life, gang members usually fought over nothing in particular, the victims of their own raging hormones.

What had happened, Rainey learned upon accessing a copy of Beau Flynn's rap sheet, was that in early September Beau was hanging at the Grocery Cart with his "bros," including Aaron Iturra. While Aaron was not a member of the gang, he was there to watch out for Beau. When *Jack Blessing* happened to come in to buy something, all hell broke loose.

"Heard you snitched on me, man," Beau shouted at Jack.

"What?" Jack replied, not knowing what Beau was talking about.

"You told 'the man' I gave you that gun off the burglary."

"I didn't!" Jack retorted. His heart started to race.

"Yeah, man, and the cops busted me for it."

"Look, Beau," Jack continued, desperate now, "I never—"

Aaron came over and put his hand on Beau's sleeve. "Hey, come on, Beau—" but Beau pushed Aaron away and pulled a knife. Quickly, he turned back to Blessing and slashed at his stomach, cutting through his jacket and scratching his skin with the blade.

The owner of the Grocery Cart had seen the assault in the making and had already called 911. Sirens screaming, cops arrived on the scene before Beau could do any further damage. Beau was arrested and when cops asked him if anyone else had participated in the assault against Blessing, he identified Aaron, who was also arrested. Aaron couldn't believe it! He was there to protect the kid and he winds up getting charged!

"What am I supposed to do?" Aaron asked Janyce when he was finally released into her charge. "Beau needs help, Mom, but if I finger him, he'll go back to jail. You know he has a record."

"Frankly, Aaron, that's not your problem. He got himself into this mess. You tried to stop it. Seems to me you did everything you could."

After much soul-searching, Aaron got really practical. *There's no way I'm going to jail for a scuzbucket like Beau*, he thought.

Aaron called Officer Richard Grimes of the Department of Public Safety and told him that Beau Flynn was responsible for assaulting Jack Blessing with a knife. Since Flynn was on parole from the MacLaren Juvenile Detention Center at the time of the assault, his parole was revoked and he was returned to MacLaren pending trial. In return, charges against Aaron were dropped. He was scheduled to testify against Beau in the assault case when he was murdered.

"I was very upset about this," Mary continued, "because I believed that Beau didn't do the scratching at the Grocery Cart. It took me a while to come to terms with that. See, emotionally, during the next two weeks before Beau went back to MacLaren, we got along better than ever. And, Beau thought that he was doing good. All I could think was, why is this happening? And then the kids would continue to come over. Then my dog got really sick and died."

Again with the dog! Mary must have recalled how her dog back in Cleveland got her kicked out of town.

"In the course of this two weeks," Mary continued, "I know I said that Aaron couldn't testify against Beau. I know I said it in front of this group of kids."

She didn't like Aaron, and couldn't believe his betrayal. *How can he hurt me this way?* Mary thought. "Cause I had asked Aaron to keep an eye out for Beau. I didn't ask Aaron to baby-sit him twenty-four hours a day. I just asked that if he heard of anything, either to let me know or to tell Beau he was screwing up."

"Try to keep him out of trouble?" Rainey nodded sympathetically.

"Try to keep him out of trouble," she repeated. "And, part of my feelings about Aaron in the last couple weeks is that he stood right there, *right there*, and let all of this happen." And she told Jim Elstad, Wayde Hudson and Joe Brown how angry she was at Aaron.

"And, one day last week I knew they had a thirty-eight handgun. I saw it. They had it at my house and I told them to get it out of my house."

"They being who?" Raynor cut in.

"They being Joe Brown. All three of them were actually there. Brown, Wayde Hudson and Jim Elstad."

"And, this is in the week just prior to the homicide?" asked Rainey, trying to get it straight in his mind.

"Yes. Yes," Mary answered emphatically. "Joe and these kids would talk, you know . . ."

"Talking tough?" Rainey interrupted.

Mary nodded. "Talking tough. Talking bad. They didn't like Aaron because of what he did to Beau, or what they felt he did, what we all felt he did to Beau. They didn't like him because of what he did to me. The hurt there. And they didn't like him because they thought he set his demons on them."

Demons? What was this, *Rosemary's Baby*?

"You mean like some kind of satanic thing or something?"

"Yes."

"So, there was a lot of stuff they were unhappy with Aaron about?"

"Yeah. But I never thought that any of this was serious. They would, you know, say, you know, that they were gonna go beat him up. They were gonna go *cap* [shoot] him. And, they had a plan where they were gonna cap him on his way to pick up his girlfriend at the market. And I said, 'I don't want to hear this, you know, you guys.' And, they shut up about it. And then on Monday morning, early, early Monday morning—"

"Which Monday was that, Mary?" Raynor interrupted.

"The Monday Aaron was killed."

"Go on," said Raynor.

"In the middle of the night there's a knock on my door. Joe Brown and Jim Elstad are standing there. They said they had just done it."

"Done what?" Rainey asked, knowing the answer like a good interrogator should.

"And Jim said that they've killed Aaron," Mary confirmed, and Rainey nodded.

"I just didn't believe these guys could do it, you know?" Mary asked incredulously. "These are kids I had *in my home*. I just didn't believe they had the guts to do it."

"What happened after that?"

"I got my clothes on real quick, hopped in our pickup and took Joe home. On the way there, Joe wanted me to drive him by the river so he could get rid of the gun.

So I took him over on River Avenue under the underpass, under the Beltline, and stopped and he went down. He was carrying a cigarette and I saw him go as far as the water's edge, and then, it was too dark to see him any further. He was gone for maybe a minute, maybe two minutes. Then he came back up and got in the truck and I took him on to his house over off of Maxwell and dropped him off. And he give me a hug and said, 'See you tomorrow, Mom.' And I went home."

Mary paused, looked down, then looked up at Rainey and said earnestly, "I didn't believe that they had actually done this even though my common sense should have told me better, 'cause, you know, we went to get rid of a gun." *You dumb ass*, she thought. And when she got home, she told her husband John what had happened.

Rainey wanted to know what Joe had told her about the shooting.

"Joe said that it was him and Jim went in there and Joe was rifling through the bitch's purse."

"The bitch," meaning Aaron's girlfriend, Carrie. Mary continued: "And Aaron turned his head like he was waking up or something and Jim never hesitated. He just capped his ass right in the head."

In order to catch someone in a lie, go over their story again. And that's what Rainey did.

"Okay. So, you get back, you drop Joe off at the house. You tell your husband John that these guys say they just capped Aaron. Then what happens?"

"My husband says, 'No they didn't. They're just telling you that.' And I said, 'Well, why did they tell me that?' And he says, 'Well, they think they're big and bad. And they're trying to impress Beau and they're trying to impress you!' I said, 'You're right.' It sounded reasonable to me. And John and I went to bed. And the next thing I know, John's coming in and telling me, 'There's three cops out here.' "

"This is when Detective Raynor came to question you?" Rainey asked.

"Yes," Mary replied. "And then you guys told me that Aaron had been shot. I thought somebody else did it, and the kids were capitalizing on it, trying to take the, uh, you know . . ."

"Credit for it?" Rainey said, finishing the sentence.

"Credit for it," Mary agreed.

"So when we showed up at the house, and we let you know this is happening and we're asking for information—"

"I thought Beau did it. I really did."

"And we told you, I think at that time, that we had already checked and Beau was in custody at the time of the murder."

Mary nodded.

"So what's your reason for not having told us the whole story right then and there, Mary?"

"Number one, I didn't believe they were capable of that. Number two, I was afraid for my safety, and my son's safety. I figured if these kids could murder, they could do me and they could do Beau."

"Okay. So going back even before that when you gave Crazy Joe a ride to the river 'cause he asks you to do that so he can get rid of the gun. From a lot of people's perspective that would suggest that there really is some truth here to what these guys are claiming. That they had just done Aaron. Why is it that you didn't attach more weight to what they were saying?"

Or, put another way, why was Mary such a moron that she refused to believe she was handling the murder weapon in a capital murder case?

"I just didn't believe them," Mary answered. "I just couldn't conceive of them doing that. I guess part of me was kinda in shock. Like, 'Damn!' You know? And then trying to weed out the wheat from the chaff."

But what really took her aback was that neither Elstad nor Brown looked shaken. They had just killed a man and they looked like they were out for a midnight walk. Both cops knew that such behavior was consistent with psychopaths, a breed of human apart, who felt no guilt for their crimes.

"Did you see any blood on anybody?" Rainey wondered.

"There was no blood."

"Did you make a point of looking for it?" Rainey pressed, leaning forward and touching Mary's arm, trying to crowd her into the corner he had placed her in.

"Yeah. And riding in the truck, I couldn't smell the gun," Mary smoothly answered, leaning forward and meeting Rainey's steely gaze. "And I'm thinking, 'They're bullshitting me.' "

Raynor had a question.

"When you were in the car, Mary, and going to the river . . ."

"Yes?"

". . . where did Joe carry the gun?"

"I'm not sure, but I think it was in the front of his pants."

Rainey, though, wanted to pin down the make of the murder weapon.

"Describe the gun for us as best you can."

"Thirty-eight wheel gun," said Mary in clipped tones. "Had wooden handles, wooden-like stock and stock grip."

She talks like a gangster and knows guns like one, Rainey thought.

"And the rest of it was blue steel," Mary added. "Maybe a three-and-a-half, four-inch barrel. Top length."

"Any idea what brand the gun was?" Rainey persisted.

"Maybe Smith and Wesson."

"A Smith and Wesson or something else?"

"Maybe a Ruger. They told me it was a thirty-eight. The week before, I knew they had a thirty-eight and, I just believed it to be the same gun."

"Did this look like the same gun they had the week before?" Raynor interjected.

Mary said that it did indeed, that Joe Brown had taken custody of the gun the week before and Joe Brown showed her the gun when the boys came to her house after the murder. As for getting rid of it, "That happened after we were in the car and we were going down River Road. Joe said, 'I'm gonna throw this gun in the river.' "

"When you got down by the bridge, did Joe tell you where to stop?"

Rainey was trying to see if Mary had any complicity in dumping the murder weapon.

"Joe directed me where to go," she answered smoothly.

"Or was there conversation between the two of you?"

"Joe directed me where to go down River Avenue 'cause I wasn't familiar with that road. But, I knew it had to go down in there somewhere 'cause I drive over the Beltline and see people with their boats. And, I see the sheep on the other side going right down to the river. And he told me to pull in, as we went under the underpass he said, told me where to stop. I guess you call it the boat ramp side. And, I stopped right there on the road, on the corner. And I said, 'Go do it.' And he jumped out and ran down to the river. He was gone maybe a minute, maybe two, then he came back up and got in the truck and said, 'It's gone.' "

"So, whose idea was it to get rid of the gun?" Rainey persisted.

"Joe's."

"Did he say why he needed to do that?"

"Well, not in so many words, but it was implied, I think, because they told me that they had just shot Aaron."

"So, your understanding was just that he's getting rid of the gun because it's evidence that could be used against him?"

"Yeah."

"Okay. So when, when Crazy Joe comes back up from the river, does he have any water on him at all? Or, does it look like he's waded or anything?"

"Nope."

Rainey was trying to establish whether Brown threw the weapon out in the river, which could be pretty far out depending upon the strength of his arm. Otherwise, if he walked in, he could only go as far as he could stand. In any case, the cop knew that a search would be launched for the murder weapon and wanted to pin down where it was in the river.

"And, that's another thing," Mary continued. "I wasn't even sure that he had gotten rid of it. I thought maybe he was lying."

"Why would you think that he didn't get rid of the gun?"

" 'Cause I had my window open, and I didn't hear a splash."

"So you just weren't convinced he'd done it, huh?"

Mary nodded.

"Please speak up for the tape."

"No."

"No, what?"

Mary sighed.

"I just wasn't convinced that Joe had dumped the gun."

Rainey made some notes on his yellow foolscap pad, then looked up.

"So when Jim and Crazy Joe come to your house, and tell you that they've just capped Aaron, who's doing the talking?"

"Both. But, not out of fear or excitement. They were both talking real calm."

Just like a psychopath, Rainey thought.

"And they said, 'We just capped his ass.' I said, 'Who did?' And Jim said, 'I did.' "

"And then, at that point Jim leaves?"

"Uh huh. And Joe runs out with him, then Joe comes back and I said, 'I'll take you home.' "

"Was there any conversation at that time regarding how exactly the murder occurred?"

"No. No."

"So the information about Crazy Joe going through the purse, did that come out in a later conversation?"

"Yeah."

"When was that conversation?" Raynor wondered.

"I think that one came out in the truck with Joe. He said that he was going through the bitch's purse, and Aaron turned his head and Jim never hesitated. He went, 'Pooooh!'"

"How'd they get in the room?" Rainey continued.

"They went through the garage door."

"*They* said that or *one* of them said that?"

"Joe said that."

And motive? While the law didn't require it, Rainey knew that motive helped to convict.

"Did you ask Joe why they killed Aaron that night?"

"No, 'cause I didn't think they did it. I couldn't believe it."

Mary sounded extremely convincing.

"So, what was your understanding from either Jim or Joe about who was actually at Aaron's place when the killing took place?"

That was crucial. With both boys on the scene, it would be two murder charges instead of one.

"My understanding from Joe Brown was that Joe Brown was there and Jim Elstad."

"So, do you know how they got to and from Aaron's house?"

Translation: Was there a getaway car with a driver we can also charge?

"On foot. I just concluded that they did it on foot."

"What else can you remember Joe told you during the car ride?"

"He said something about if Jim gets caught, he'll say he did it."

"That he would take responsibility for killing Aaron?"

"Right. And I said something about, 'Well, do you really think they're gonna catch Jim?' And he said, 'Nah.' And that also led me to believe that nothing had actually happened."

"Did Joe indicate to you that he knew that when he went to Aaron's place that night that Aaron was gonna die?"

"No."

"So, is it possible from what they told you then, that when they went there, it wasn't specifically with the plan of killing him? But that it just happened while they were there?"

In which case, it wouldn't be premeditated and the death penalty would be off the table.

Mary looked perplexed. She shook her head. "I don't know. I don't have those answers. They didn't tell me. And I wasn't there."

Rainey leaned in toward Mary and without thinking, she sat back in her chair.

"Was there any information from these guys or anybody else for that matter, that anything was taken from Aaron's room?"

"No."

"Then what was Crazy Joe going through her purse for?"

"Looking for her wallet."

"And what was he gonna do with that?"

"Take the money!" Mary exclaimed, not bothering to hide the impatience.

"Is that what you know or are you guessing?"

"That's just what I figured."

"Mary, since then, since that morning, have you talked to any of these people?" Raynor interjected.

"I've talked to everybody since then, except Wayde Hudson," she answered quickly.

She was glad Raynor, whom she trusted, had begun to question her. She felt that Rainey was just trying to trap her into some sort of admission.

"You've talked to Jim?"

She nodded.

"I talked to Jim on the phone on Monday while he was at the hospital and his sister was in labor."

Jim Elstad's sister Angel had been pregnant and had just given birth to a healthy baby boy. Angel had stopped by that night. She recalled that the girl had been too pregnant to get out of the car.

"Did you talk about the incident?" Raynor continued, substituting the less emotional word "incident" for "murder."

"No. He called up and told me that Aaron Iturra had been shot. And I went, 'So?' "

Gee, she's being real emotional about this, Rainey thought.

"See, this is all part of what's mind-blowing to me," Mary continued. "He said that the police had been there and put stuff on his hands, and there was nothing wrong with his hands. And then we talked about Angel. And at that point, when he told me nothing came up on his hands, I kind of thought, 'Well, he didn't do it.' 'Cause what I know about it is what I got off the TV, and that stuff changes colors right away. You know? So, this was part of me not believing he did it."

"How about Joe Brown? Have you talked to him since then?"

"I've talked to Joe every day. And, Joe just keeps calling me and telling me the cops are jammin' him. And I said, 'If you didn't do anything, you have nothing to be guilty of.' He said, 'Yeah, you're right.' And then, it was kinda like, yesterday when Angel told me that Jim did it and that I needed to tell the police, I knew then that they did it for sure."

"Well, let's talk about that conversation with Angel then," said Rainey, leaning back in his seat. "When did that occur? Did she call you or . . ."

"No, she came by on her way home from the hospital with Christopher, her baby."

"Okay. So, the baby and Angel are there. You're there. Is anybody else present during this conversation?"

"No."

"And what does Angel tell you?"

"Angel walks back up under the carport and I look her right in the eye and I go, 'These guys didn't do this.' And she said, 'Jim did it.' And that floored me. I was still trying to believe they hadn't done it until Angel looked me in the eye and said, 'Jim did it. That's why you need to tell the police we were here Sunday night visiting until about eleven thirty.' "

In other words, Rainey thought, "Gang Mom" was supposed to provide Elstad and Brown with an alibi. They were visiting her instead of murdering Aaron.

"She was supposed to call me later in the afternoon, and I was supposed to go over and see the baby. And I assume that that was to talk to her about what had happened. And then, I had the phone call from you asking me what time they were here till. And I said, 'Eleven thirty. Eleven fifteen or eleven thirty.' And, I hung up and I said, 'No. I can't continue to do this.' "

Nope, Mary was a good citizen. She wouldn't lie for one of her kids. But it was okay for Aaron to lie to protect Beau. She failed to see the irony.

Rainey said, "So when I call you later, after Angel has just spoken with you, the information that you gave me about them visiting the house earlier in the evening on that Sunday . . ."

"Was incorrect."

"And that lie was based on what Angel had asked you to do."

Mary nodded.

"Why would she ask you to do that as opposed to somebody else?"

"Well, because she was trying to make sure I said the same thing so there would be no questions."

"She was trying to line up her story, then?"

Mary nodded.

"So you and Angel haven't had any further conversations about the killing?"

"No."

"No. And in terms of Jim Elstad, other than when he called you from the hospital, have you had any further contact with him?"

"No."

"If I could back up for just a moment?" Raynor asked.

"Sure," Rainey replied.

"In fact, were Elstad and Brown ever at your house on that evening till eleven fifteen or eleven thirty?"

"I don't think so."

"So you don't have any further contact with Jim El-stad other than that phone conversation?"

"That's right."

"Was there anything distinctive about the gun in terms of damage, or any kind of wear pattern to it, or anything like that?" Rainey asked, getting back to ba-sics.

"I never held the gun, I never fired the gun, didn't even want to pay attention to the gun," answered Mary emphatically. "Had all this not come down with my son, I'd've picked up the phone and called the police and told them these kids got a gun. I know how gang members get. They all sit around and talk nonsense."

"Did the gun look newer to you versus beat-up or anything? What did it look like to you?"

"The gun looked like a thirty-eight."

"Color?"

"It looked like a black gun. Or the correct terminol-ogy, a blue gun."

Mary really knew her weapons. Only someone fa-miliar with revolvers would know that what seems like a black color on gun metal is actually blue, the result of a bluing process done at the factory.

"In terms of the numerous contacts you had with Crazy Joe after the killing, did he continue to make statements to you about the killing?"

"No. He made statements about getting caught."

"What were those statements?"

"That they'd never really catch him."

"Why did he think that?"

"I don't know why he thought that."

"Was there any conversation with you and Joe about

him feeling like he needed to take additional precautions to keep from getting caught?"

"No."

"Did Crazy Joe ever express any remorse about what had happened?"

"No! They didn't act, they didn't act panicked. They didn't act upset about it at all. I thought they should. I thought there should be, at least, you know, some remorse. And they never said. 'Oh, I feel bad. I feel bad for me, I feel bad for Aaron. I feel bad for his family.' They never said none of that."

"But how can you be sure of what *they* said if the only one you had any real contact with was Crazy Joe?"

"Joe yesterday . . ." Mary began, then her voice trailed off as she realized she had been caught in a lie. Without giving her a chance to explain, Rainey continued, "Mary, it's still not clear to me, in terms of at least Crazy Joe anyway. After the killing. Did he make other statements to you regarding the killing?"

"We talked on the phone. No. He was calling mostly to see how I was."

"Did he ever tell you not to say anything to the police?"

"He asked me what I was telling the police 'cause I had told him the police were at my house. And I said I told them nothing. And he said, 'Good. Don't.' And, that's all he said about it."

"I'm gonna have to switch this tape over. The time right now is 1344 hours," said Rainey, shutting off the machine.

While the tape was being changed, Mary went to the bathroom. Rainey had a chance to talk with Michaud and told him of the substance of the interrogation so far, because that's what it was, an interrogation, pure and simple. While neither cop was expecting Mary Thompson to confess to killing Aaron Iturra, they knew now that their instincts had been right. Mary was involved right up to her big fat neck.

"Okay, send a detective out to rattle Angel Elstad's chain," Michaud advised.

"She'll never give up her brother Jim."

"Maybe not, but maybe there's something else she'll say that'll help us. And get warrants for Elstad and Brown. I want 'em brought in."

SEVEN

MOST TIMES WHEN DEATH occurs, the bereaved can count on family to help out, but in Janyce's case, that would not happen.

Janyce Iturra's family lived in Portland. There were sisters and brothers there, a mother and a father still alive, but there had never been anything between them. To Janyce, they were a narcissistic bunch. To expect anything from them would be to set herself up for further disappointment and grief. Janyce's opinion was that her kids wouldn't even know their grandmother if she walked down the road.

If there was one positive thing about Aaron's death, it just reinforced in Janyce's mind that she wasn't going to allow things to happen to her kids that had happened to her growing up. *I love my kids with all my heart*, Janyce thought. *And they know that. And growing up, I never even knew that was a possibility.*

Like her kids, Janyce was grieving. And like her kids, she was angry too. She wanted Aaron's killer to die in the worst way. But there was nothing she could do about that anger because she was the one who had to remain in control. Revenge right now would just prevent her from going on. Better to push it down. She'd bring it out when the time was right. What was that old Sicilian proverb that she had heard someplace? Oh, yes, she remembered.

Revenge is a dish best served cold.

While her revenge lay thriving in her conscience, there were funeral arrangements to make. That was going to cost $5,000 and she didn't know where she would get the money to cover the costs. And she needed help with Aaron . . .

"Tina, I can't do everything by myself," she told her daughter. Tina knew that.

"I'm going to have to ask you to grow up quick, baby. I want you to go shopping and pick out something he would like." Janyce was asking her oldest daughter to pick out the clothes her son would be buried in.

Aaron no longer had to worry about school, but his siblings did. The kids had been out of school since the murder. Time to go back. She needed to get as much normality back into their lives as possible.

Living arrangements. Since the murder, they'd been living away from home, but she couldn't impose on her friend any longer so she had to make plans to take her brood of five—no, *four*, she had to remind herself, *four without Aaron*—back home. Back to the house where her son had been murdered.

How do you clean blood off walls?

Actually, you don't. Because of its organic origin, blood seeps into the very fabric of the wall. Wipe it as much as you want, paint over it with oil- instead of water-based paint to hide its color, whatever you do, forevermore the blood will always be part of the house. Some part of Aaron will always be there.

And so, as Tina picked out her brother's funeral garments, as Janyce simultaneously made plans to bury her son and move her brood back home, just miles away, the cops picked at the detritus of her life and began the second part of the questioning of the one woman who seemed to hold the key to what had really happened the night of Aaron Iturra's death.

Despite their inaccuracy, "NYPD Blue" has very dramatic interrogation scenes. Usually, the suspect sits in the green interrogation room with the two-way mirror, at a scarred, pitted table. He sneers at "Sipowicz," while "Simone" shouts out questions. Then, "Sipowicz" 's hand lashes out like a whip to slap the suspect who clams up.

Let's face it, really dramatic stuff. Real life instead of reel life?

Not.

It takes hours for a cop to get the suspect settled and comfortable enough to begin to talk about what really happened, and then, if the cops are very lucky, to make a confession. While there may be some cool revelations that come out during interrogations, for the most part, they are cluttered with boring information. In Mary's case, it was her fixation on dogs.

During the second part of her interrogation, Mary went on and on and on and on about her beloved dog Lars. It was Lars this and Lars that, Lars went to the vet, Lars had intravenous therapy, Lars got a new kennel, Lars had a tumor, until finally, thank God, Lars died and they could get back to what was really important, Aaron's death.

Mary related better to her dog's death than Aaron's.

You didn't have to be an animal lover to find that interesting.

As she went on to describe Lars's funeral out back of her house, where Joe Brown dug the beloved pooch a grave, Rainey steered the conversation back to the murder weapon, the gun that Elstad, Brown and Larry Martin, Mary admitted, passed around the week before the murder.

The Saturday after Lars died, they all came over.

"Larry came over with Jim," Mary recalled. "Because Wayde, Larry, Angel and this Linda all stayed at Linda's house the night before 'cause Angel was *smacking* on [flirting with] Larry. And Angel was wanting me to fix things up with her and Larry. And Larry was going, 'I can't do it. I can't do it. I can't do it.' Angel was pregnant out to here."

"Then what happened?"

"Larry came over. Wayde and Linda were there for a little bit. And Angel. Anyway, Larry and Joe ended up staying. And they all knew that, you know, I told them Lars died. And, I told everybody that we thought it was cancer. And Larry said that Aaron's 'evil' caused the cancer."

"Evil?" Rainey questioned.

"Larry is one of these that's totally convinced that Aaron's demons were after him," Mary answered.

"Is he pretty gullible, you think? Larry?" Rainey asked matter-of-factly, which was a credit to his poker face considering how the situation really warranted sarcasm.

"Larry? I think Larry's pretty *baked* [stoned]. He called me and said that him and Aaron had been in a fight on Thursday. And he goes, 'Mary, what did I do on Thursday?' And I said, 'Well, I don't know.' 'I'd remember if I got in a fight 'cause I like to fight.' But I wasn't with him on Thursday. 'Cause he had went to a party or something Aaron had and puked all over Aaron's bedroom and was quite pleased with himself for doing that. I guess that was the weekend before this last weekend that he was over at Aaron's house, and they had been drinking beers, and Aaron had pizza, and he ate the pizza and got sick and puked all over Aaron's bedroom. 'All over his stuff' was the way he put it."

"So when did you have this conversation with Jim?" Raynor asked.

"It had to be on Saturday 'cause I didn't see anybody on Sunday."

"Okay. You remember the gist of that conversation?" Raynor continued.

"I said that it was either poisoning or cancer that killed Lars. Somebody said, and I don't remember who it was, 'Here's another thing Aaron did.' I says, 'No, you can't blame this on Aaron because we're not sure what he died of. All I know is he's dead.' And, I don't even remember if Jim was there for sure. I really don't, now that I think about it. I was very, very upset. These guys know how upset I was the day Beau was arrested. I was really about the same."

"Right."

"But I wasn't blaming anybody," Mary added hastily. "I was blaming the frigging vet for not saving Lars."

The conversation was straying from the mark. Rainey needed to turn things around, and fast, before he lost the momentum of the interrogation. So he gently came in with questions about the gun, trying to trace how it wound up being used to kill Aaron. The idea was to see how many hands it had passed through; how many accessories to murder there might be. But, what with Beau's troubles, and the grief over Lars's death, her recollection was hazy at best. Rainey moved on.

"So jumping up to Monday morning, after Aaron is dead, these guys show up. Joe has the gun at that time? Is that right?"

"Yes."

"Does Joe have it in his hand when they walk up? Or, does he pull it out of someplace, or what?"

"In front of his pants."

"So he lifted the top of his shirt to show you the gun tucked into his waistband?"

"I think he took it out once. See, Angel was in labor, I was dealing with that and then I went to the door, and it went back in his pants."

"So you mean you were busy helping Angel when they showed up? But didn't you tell one of us during the first interview that Angel drove up in a car, that she never got out?"

"No. She never did."

"So what do you mean that you were so busy dealing with Angel in labor that it was hard to pay attention when two guys show up with a gun tucked in their belt?"

Mary thought quickly. "I was dealing with everybody at the door, getting them to leave."

"Remember what they were wearing that night?" Raynor interjected.

"I can't remember. I didn't turn the light on while Jim was there. And, they're all calm and kicked-back about it."

"How about Joe?" Raynor asked.

"Had on orange shorts."

"Were they sweat-type shorts or pants or the baggy kind?"

"Baggy denim. They were orange denim. And I thought, that's close enough to red that I wouldn't wear it if I was claiming what he was claiming."

Mary meant it would be the wrong gang color to wear during a killing. He should be wearing the gang's colors instead. Mary described the way the two boys were dressed that night.

"Is it possible," Rainey wanted to know, "if Larry Martin could have been with them and involved in the killing?"

"Yeah. I didn't see Larry. I had talked to Larry earlier on the phone. Larry and I talked on Monday and see, Larry went underground on Monday. And he called and told me he was scared. And I says, 'Where's Wayde?' And he said that he thought that Wayde and Linda were gonna hook it up (meet) and go to Seattle."

"Well, if Larry wasn't involved in the murder, what was he worried about? I don't understand."

"Before he went underground, a detective, Dick Grimes, told him, 'You better pull up your pants. You better start walking the line because you're next.'"

Gang members typically wear their pants down off their waists in such a way that it indicates gang membership. Grimes was supposedly warning Larry that if he didn't start wearing his clothes normally, he'd be a target for whomever had killed Aaron.

"And so, he thought he was gonna get killed," Mary continued.

"But, he knew all these people. Why not just go to

the source and say, 'Man, you know, I'm hearing this crap. What's going on?' "

"Because I don't think Larry thought they did it, either. 'Cause I think Larry thought it was bigger than this."

Aha, back to the theory of Sonny, the hit man from Portland.

"There was a lot of publicity of course after the homicide in the media Monday, Tuesday, Wednesday, today. Has any of that publicity prompted anybody that you know of to, you know, make any comments to you about the killing and what's going on?"

"About?"

"Just their involvement or what they know about it. Who else would they have confided in?"

"Who?"

"The people that are responsible for the killing! Or have firsthand knowledge."

"You mean the two that went?"

"Right."

"I think Angel knows. I think Cameron knows. I think Larry knows."

"You think they'd tell Larry? Or do you think he was there?"

"I think they'd tell him. I don't know what Larry knows. It's so hard to tell with Larry."

"Anybody else?" Rainey continued.

"Maybe Wayde?" Raynor added.

"Maybe they called Wayde."

"Let's say we have information that you provided the gun. Okay? Let's say we sit down with Crazy Joe or Elstad or somebody that says, 'Well, I don't know what

Mary's trying to pull here, but she's the one who gave us the gun.' Is there any truth to that?"

"No."

"No way?"

"None. No way in Frosty's butt."

"Or that it might have come through you or anything like that? Right?"

"Right. None."

"Or," Rainey continued casually, "let's say the statement is made from one of these other people that, 'Well, the only reason why we did the killing is 'cause Mary asked us to.' "

Bingo! It was right out there. Now Mary knew for sure what Rainey thought.

"See, that's where part of my guilty feelings come into this. I didn't say, 'I want you guys to get together, pick one, go kill him. Go do this.' "

"What statements did you make that, that you think that they could have somehow interpreted—"

"That first day that Beau had been arrested. I know I had to have said I wished he were dead. I mean I was out of control."

"Okay."

"It was all I could do to get home, drive myself home from Willamette High School after Beau was arrested."

"Do you think it's likely that you made statements like, you know, 'People who *narc* [inform] get killed'?"

"Oh, yeah."

"I mean that's a pretty typical reaction when your son is arrested."

"Oh, yeah. Yeah."

"Okay. And so, if somebody says, 'We did this because Mary told us to and she promised that we would get something for it, money, whatever . . .' "

Mary laughed at the absurdity of it all.

"I'm sorry," Rainey apologized sincerely, "I'm just trying to throw out all the possibilities here that we might later, you know, have thrown at us by some of these other people. Is there any truth—"

"No. None," Mary interrupted.

"Was anything given to anybody, you know . . ."

"No!"

". . . that might have even been mistaken for or in lieu of payment for . . ."

"No!"

Mary vehemently denied putting anyone up to killing Aaron so that he couldn't testify against Beau in the Grocery Cart knifing incident. "But I did bring it up about the hearing coming up that Aaron can't go and say what he said in that police report," Mary added.

"And by that you meant he can't be saying that kind of junk against Beau?"

"Right. Right."

"That ain't right."

"Right. It's not right. He's lying."

"Okay."

"He lied in the police report. He lied. He cannot continue to tell these lies."

"Okay. So when this statement is made, is there a hearing that was about to occur or that was pending?"

"No. There was none scheduled."

"Okay."

Mary stopped and listened.

"I keep hearing something going click, click, click," she said. "I'm wondering if it's all my stuff."

"It could be my radio," Rainey said, pulling out his

walkie talkie and adjusting one of the knobs.

"Oh."

"That probably is what it is. If his radio is going, every time it's keyed it would click."

" 'Cause I have a little TV in here," said Mary, pointing to her purse. "And I have my pull-out stereo from my car. My Walkman. You know, that kind of stuff."

"Okay."

"But, I never said to do it, to kill him."

"Okay. And did you say, you know, I'm asking this question just like we have before, did you say anything indirectly which you intended to cause them to kill Aaron?"

"No. But indirectly, I worry about that. You know, 'He can't testify. I hate him.' "

"Okay. But we're talking about intent here, what you intended by an indirect statement . . ."

"No," said Mary again, emphatically denying any involvement in a plot to kill Aaron. "I never intended anything that I said to get Aaron killed."

"Okay, so what is your best understanding of why Aaron was killed?"

"My best understanding of why Aaron was killed, because of him being a part of Beau going back to MacLaren, the hurt he was putting me through by the stuff he was saying about Beau in the police reports and because he had stole from me. And it could have something to do with them thinking that maybe Lars was poisoned by Aaron. And because of the demons."

"Okay."

"Aaron's demons."

Mary went on to recall how some of the kids who hung around her place had discussions about "hurting

Aaron," by "getting him" as he went to pick up his girlfriend. "They were gonna run up and cap him twice and keep on running." But she couldn't remember who said that. Then Mary advanced the theory that Aaron might have been killed because he set Larry up for a robbery at school.

Rainey leaned in closer to Mary, crowding her into the corner. "Who was it who was basically talking about putting the hurt on Aaron?"

"All of them."

"When we say 'All of them,' I mean somebody who was serious, somebody who's just really got a hard-on about it."

"I couldn't even really say that these guys really had a hard-on about it. They didn't come off like that. They weren't consumed with even half their waking hours trying to figure out how to do Aaron in."

But somebody was, Rainey thought, otherwise we wouldn't be having this conversation. Instead, he said, "Amongst this group are there some that are talking junk more than others about this issue?"

"No. They were all talking."

"When we say 'all,' we're talking Jim Elstad, Wayde Hudson?"

"Yes."

"Larry Martin?"

"Yes."

"Crazy Joe?"

"Yes."

"Is Angel even contributing to some of this stuff?"

"Yes."

"Linda?"

"Linda said she didn't know about it, but her and Angel were pretty tight."

"What about Cameron? Cameron talking crap?"

"They were all talking crap."

"Ric, can you think of anything else?"

Mary trusted Raynor a hell of a lot more than Rainey. Based on her previous experiences with Raynor, Mary felt that he would acknowledge and advocate her point of view. She seemed to be more open answering his questions.

"Have any of these people ever given you any indication that they have discussed this in a roundabout way through letters, through phones or anything with Beau, and that Beau is in any way involved in this?" said Raynor.

"I have no indication that Beau's involved," Mary replied quickly.

"Is there any indication," Raynor continued, "that Beau even knew about Aaron being killed?"

"No."

"Getting back to that same discussion we had a little bit earlier about 'what ifs,' " Rainey broke in. "Is there anything that any of these people could say that you somehow furnished them any kind of support to make this happen? 'Support' meaning you gave them a sketch of the place [Aaron's house]. Or that you drove them to and from the location. In other words, other than the gun, is there anything else that you might have assisted in disposing . . ."

"No!"

". . . of on their behalf?"

"The only support they got from me was immediately after when I took Joe home and dropped him by the river, and then waited for him and took him to his house."

Rainey wanted to know if at any time during the interview, Mary had deliberately tried to mislead them. "So there was no conscious effort on your part to . . ."

"Throw you guys off?"

"Right."

"No. There was not. Even knowing what I know, I still am having a hard time believing it."

"Why did you decide to finally come forward, Mary?" Rainey wondered.

" 'Cause I figured it out yesterday when Angel looked me in the eye and said, 'Jim did it.' And everything just kinda fit together."

"Were you really afraid that someone else would talk first and you'd be left holding the bag?"

"No! No! There's a lot of things that went through my mind. I know how much time you guys put in solving cases. You guys are busting your ass. I had to tell you. I tried to get a hold of Ric yesterday. And it wasn't meant to be 'cause I guess he was trying to get a hold of me and I was grounded to the house. I just had to do it."

"Is there anything you told us today where you weren't totally truthful? Anything you've held back from us we need to know about?"

"Not that I can think of, feel right now, today, that it's been all put out there. Win, lose or draw."

"What, what do you think should happen to you, Mary, for what you've done? I mean, do you think you should be charged with a crime?"

"I'm sure that there's room there to be charged with a crime. I was totally stupid all the way around in this.

I think my major crime is being flipped out for the last three weeks 'cause of everything that happened and not paying attention."

"Would it, would it be fair to say that you coming in here today and sitting down and cooperating with us like you have, is maybe an effort on your part to try to set things straight?"

"Yeah!"

"Make things right?"

"To tell the truth."

"Okay."

"You know, I can't bring Aaron back by being here. And I can't change what I've done by being here. But it's telling the truth, and that's what needs to happen. Everybody needs to tell the truth."

"Okay."

"Isn't that what we've been asking?" said Raynor earnestly. "Isn't that what I said over and over is all we want is the truth and nothing more?"

"Right."

"Do you feel that you're willing to keep helping and keep telling the truth, and keep helping us try to get to the bottom of this?" Raynor continued.

"Yes. Yes. Very much so."

"Okay, anything else you can think of, Mary, right now? I mean, there may be further questions that are gonna come up or something like that. But at least at this point, do you feel comfortable with what you said so far?" Rainey asked.

"I still worry about maybe I said too much. I fear for my family."

The cops were satisfied that they had gotten all they could out of Mary. The tape recorder was turned off.

While Mary and Raynor chatted, Rainey left the room. He came back a few minutes later, and whispered something to Raynor. *What the hell is going on?* Mary wondered.

Rainey turned back to her.

"Mary, the detective who's supervising this case thought there was one more thing you could help us out with," said Rainey.

"Sure," Mary replied, "anything I can do."

"We'd like you to make a call."

"I'm not a snitch!" Mary declared.

"Oh, nothing like that, we just want to clarify a few points. And make the people who killed Aaron pay. You do want to do that, don't you?"

Mary nodded.

"Besides, it's just one phone call."

"Okay," Mary answered. "One call."

They started to walk out with Rainey explaining exactly what they wanted her to do. "Would you like to meet the detective supervising?"

"Sure," she said, and they ushered her over to Michaud's desk. He was on the phone with his back to her. "Yeah, yeah, I'll call you back."

He hung up the phone and turned around.

"Hello, Mary, how the heck are you?" said Michaud jauntily.

She recognized him instantly.

"Hello, Detective Michaud, nice to see you again."

"Nice to see you, Mary," and Michaud did nothing to disguise his smile.

EIGHT

In the post–World War II era, a construction firm named Levitt and Sons built small, one-family ranch houses on postage stamp-sized lots east of New York City, on Long Island. Named Levittown, the idea was to provide affordable housing to returning vets in a community within easy commuting distance of New York City.

Levitt-style houses proved so popular that other contractors across the country began building similar types of bedroom communities. Eugene was no exception to this building boom and as it turned out, Mary Thompson, her contractor husband John and her son Beau shared one of these Levitt-style houses in a middle-income community on the fringes of town.

The Thompson home may have been small at 1000 square feet with two bedrooms, but with its construction of cement, brick and wood, and its neat, square, flat roof, there was a feeling of security about the place. Floor-to-ceiling front windows gave it an open air, which wasn't surprising since Mary's house, as she'd said, was always open to Eugene's troubled teens who had joined gangs.

The cops, with Rainey supervising, set up their listening equipment on the living-room phone.

"Ready?" Rainey asked.

Mary nodded, picked up the phone and dialed Angel Elstad's number. Angel came on the line immediately and after they exchanged pleasantries, Mary got right into it. She pumped Angel for what she knew about the murder. And Angel, trusting her "Gang Mom," fell right into the trap.

"Okay, from what Jim told me is that, and I'm only telling you so don't think I'm a narc or something. I drove my car over with Jim and Joe and dropped them off near Aaron and then they went over to Aaron's house. They were in the back and they said that there was five people sitting in the house with Aaron. So that was like okay. And so Jim comes back later with Joe and they're telling me all this stuff and he goes, 'Now we're gonna try it in a little bit later.' I said, 'Okay.' And . . . your phone's not tapped, right?"

"I don't think so."

"It's like, 'cause ours isn't. But then, so they left again and we waited and waited and Jack and Cameron were here and we were visiting and chatting and then we heard this 'pop.' And all three of us stopped. We're like going, 'Wow!' You know? 'Was that it? Was that it?' We go, 'That was it.' And not even a minute later, the boys come walking in the door. And Jim's shaking, you know, going, 'I did it! I did it!' And I'm like, 'Well, how do you feel?' And he goes, 'I feel great! 'Cause you get such a thrill from it, you know?' And I'm like 'What?' And Joe is all, 'Yeah, you get a thrill from it.' And I was like, 'Okay!' And Joe had his hand open and he showed me four bullets and one shell. I was like, well, they had to have done it then. And Jim said that, you know, he got there and Aaron was like lifting up his head or something and Jim got him in the back of the head."

"Wow!"

"They watched him fall on the pillow. Jim said nobody could have survived that."

"So you knew they were gonna do this?"

"Yep," Angel confirmed, hanging herself. "Everybody kept telling them to do it. And after hearing it so many times, they did it. It was Jim who did it. It was Jim who finally did it."

"I never thought they'd do it," Mary said plaintively.

"'Cause Jim said that he talked to you on the phone and you said it needed to get done soon."

"I wasn't serious. You know that," Mary replied earnestly.

"Then after it happened we went over to your house because Jim said that he was supposed to tell you if he did it. And so we went over to your house."

"Well, you know, I was the one said I didn't want to know about it."

Every time a hole was dug further, Mary found a way out.

As the cops continued to listen, Rainey went outside to his squad car and picked up the car radio.

"Ten-four, ten-four, this is Rainey."

"Dispatcher here, Detective," the voice crackled over the radio.

"Patch me through to Michaud."

There was some clicking on the line and then the familiar voice.

"Michaud here."

"Jim, it's Les. Angel admitted to Mary that Elstad and Brown did the murder."

"Pick them up as soon as she's finished talking."

Rainey got back not more than a minute later.

"I told them," Mary was saying, "I told them they'd talk that crap over here and I'd say, 'I don't want to know about it.' "

"Yeah."

"And you were here when I said that."

"Yeah."

"Do you think Wayde knows about what happened?"

"No, I think Wayde has a vague idea, but I don't think he knows all the details. I think it's pretty much Cameron and Jack and I. To tell you the honest truth, I didn't think Jim had it in him."

"Well, I been saying that all week."

"So, I'm gonna get off here and I'll talk to you tomorrow."

"Alrighty."

"All right. Bye." The line went dead.

Rainey was all set to turn off his tape recorder and pack up his equipment when the phone rang. Mary looked at the detective.

"Answer it," Rainey said. So Mary picked up the phone on the third ring.

"Hello?" said Mary.

"Hello," said the voice on the other end of the line. It was Lisa Fentress.

"I heard you had to go downtown?" Mary asked.

"They might arrest me 'cause they think I'm withholding evidence," said Lisa, sounding obviously disturbed.

"Well, what do you know?"

"What?"

"What do you know?" Mary repeated.

"I don't know anything."

"Well, have you talked to Crazy and all that?"

"I talked to him, but I didn't talk to him about anything important."

"Well, they're just jammin' ya," Mary said calmly.

"That's all anybody talks to me about anymore. The murder. That's all I'm good for anymore. Like I'm not a real person. I just feel bad because people are calling me crying. People are calling me asking me if their kid's a gang member."

Mary chuckled.

"Everybody's calling me for everything. I don't know why people think I know so much."

"Okay, honey. Bye bye."

Mary hung up the phone. Rainey unplugged the recorder from the phone, then went out to his squad car again and called Michaud. After being filled in on the substance of the "tap," Michaud gave serious consideration to bringing Mary in for murder.

"Hang there, Les, let me call Skelton."

Michaud called Steve Skelton, the assistant district attorney who had arrived at the crime scene to assist the investigating officers. After consulting with Skelton, Michaud realized they didn't have a case against Mary.

At no time had Mary commissioned the murder. Merely suggesting that "it had to be done soon," or that after it was done to contact her was not enough to get a murder one indictment. Even a lesser charge of murder two would be hard to prove. There was no physical or forensic evidence, or any evidence for that matter, to tie her into the crime. Michaud got back to Rainey.

"What about motive, Les?"

Rainey thought that if Mary did sanction the murder it was to prevent Aaron from testifying against Beau and putting him back in jail for violating probation. But Michaud had another theory. Before he shared it with anyone, he needed to check it out.

"Listen, Les, re-interview Mary, tie up whatever loose ends you can and come in."

Michaud turned to his computer and called up the crime statistics for the city. They showed that in recent months, there had been a wave of unsolved burglaries and auto thefts. Drug dealing was also on the rise.

If his theory was right, then the death of Aaron Iturra was actually tied into the crime wave. Either way, he'd need a hell of a lot more on Mary to sustain a murder charge, let alone a conviction.

Rainey set his tape recorder down on the coffee table in Mary's living room. Mary sat next to him, Raynor on the other side. It was like any other early fall afternoon, just three people sitting around talking—except this talk was about murder.

"To the best of your knowledge, did Lisa Fentress have any involvement in Aaron's murder?" Rainey asked.

Mary said she wasn't aware she had any. She described how she met Lisa through her "Gang Awareness" seminars, and how Lisa had taken an instant liking to Mary. "She kind of 'glommed' on to me," was the way Mary put it.

As for the most recent time she had spoken to Lisa, it was ". . . last night. I kept the conversation with her real short and sweet because I was trying to figure out what to do, and I didn't want her to try to sway me one way or the other."

"Really?"

Mary nodded. "I knew I had to make an independent decision. I knew I didn't want her to know if I had decided to talk to the police or not because I know that she would tell everybody else."

And Mary would get the reputation of being a "stoolie" once again.

"Anything else you can think of in terms of your contacts with Lisa concerning the homicide?"

"Well, we talked about it through the week," Mary continued, "because it was Lisa's mother who was the Victims Services advocate that was called out on it."

"Lisa's mom was?" Rainey asked in astonishment.

"Yeah. Her name is Parr. Heather Parr. She has a different last name than Lisa."

"Anything else you can think of right now, Mary?"

"No."

"Then we'll be concluding this interview regarding Lisa Fentress. The time is now 1822 hours."

Click.

While there was no evidence that Victims Services advocate Heather Parr in any way leaked information to her daughter Lisa about the Iturra killing, Lori Nelson, the Victims Services manager, removed her from the case and substituted herself instead.

Late in the day on October 6, 1994, police arrested Jim Elstad and Crazy Joe Brown for the murder of Aaron Iturra. Michaud could see that they were preening. They felt like media stars, what with all the attention the police gave them. Michaud decided to interrogate Elstad.

"So tell me what happened that night," Michaud asked Brown casually. He had changed into his "Pink

Floyd" T-shirt, the one he liked to use during interrogations. If he felt more casual, then the suspect would, too, and begin to trust him. And he'd put him in the soft interrogation room that looked like a living room, with muted lighting, sofa and coffee table.

An old cop named Fred, whom he considered to be his mentor, had taught Michaud to be patient during questioning. Fred always reminded him that suspects hated silence. "Just work the suspect," Fred would say. "Sooner or later they'll talk."

So Michaud did as his mentor had taught him. He chatted lightly with Elstad, making sure to leave a lot of silence, which Elstad happily filled in. Quickly, proudly, he admitted to being responsible for Aaron's death. It was the gang code of honor to take responsibility for their actions, especially when such actions were to enforce gang unity and honor, as they were, he claimed, in this case.

"Aaron was killed because he snitched to the cops about the knifing of the Blessing kid."

"Really?"

Silence.

"Yeah, and that like caused you guys to revoke Beau's parole and you sent him back to MacLaren."

"So?"

The silence filled the room until Elstad confessed, "We had to get Aaron for that."

"Did Mary Thompson put you up to it?" Michaud asked.

"No way," Elstad retorted. "I did it on my own. With Joe."

In the hard interrogation room down the hall, Brown was giving a similar story to Rainey.

"Beau took swipes at the kid and cut his stomach at the Grocery Cart," Brown recalled. "Then Aaron opened his mouth. We had to get him."

"We." Despite the fact that he hadn't done anything but provide moral support, Brown was prouder of their "accomplishment"—snuffing out Aaron's life—than the shooter.

"Would you show us how it happened?"

"Sure."

While Elstad remained in custody, Rainey, Michaud, Raynor and two other officers, with Crazy Joe Brown in tow, set off for the Iturra house to reenact the murder. Once there, Michaud got down on the blood-stained mattress that Aaron had once occupied, with Raynor playing the girlfriend. Brown arranged the tableau exactly as it was that night, then paced back to the door and, using his hand like a kid would, made believe it was a pistol and leveled it at Michaud's head.

"Boom!" he shouted.

Michaud rose up slowly, the way Brown said that Aaron did, then tumbled down.

Outside, Brown retraced the steps he took with Elstad as they retreated to Elstad's house. He spoke in matter-of-fact terms about what they had done, exhibiting no guilt whatsoever.

Later that night, they all stood by the banks of the river and he showed them where Mary was waiting in her truck while he threw the murder weapon and the remaining bullets into the raging water. Michaud looked around at the darkness, at the young boy who would soon be a convicted murderer and thought about the woman who was sitting comfortably in her house back in the city, the woman he believed was responsible for this death, a woman who was getting away with murder.

He should have felt cold, what with the wet fall breeze coming in off the river. Instead, he felt unusually warm and had to open his jacket to cool off.

NINE

"HEY, DID YOU HEAR, the Crips killed Iturra?"

"Oh, yeah?"

"Yeah, it's all over town."

And it was. The members of the 74 Hoover Crips, Lisa and Beau, Lennie and Wayde, all of them, had been emboldened by their killing of Aaron Iturra and were bragging about it to the members of the Eugene gang community. The death only served to give them greater status in the gang world.

During the fall of 1994, if you were a Eugene resident and your car was stolen, chances are it was a Crip. House burglarized? Crips. Your kid buying drugs? Crips. Certainly they were not responsible for all of the city's crime, but they had a hand in a good portion of it and they were running unchecked because only Michaud suspected how active they really were. To stop them meant stopping Mary.

There was a rash of drive-by shootings for which the 74 Hoover Crips took the credit. Even their own were not free from retribution.

When it got back to the gang that *Cameron Slade* might be prepared to help the cops out, a couple of the *homies* [gang members] drove by his house and pegged a couple of shots inside. No one was hurt, but Cameron got the message.

While only three days had passed since the murder, things were pretty much the same as before at Mary's house, except that there was a new excitement. Aaron's death had energized everyone. *Sam Warthan*, who wasn't a gang member but came over to visit frequently, noticed it when he dropped by one day to say "hi" to Beau. They wound up horsing around, discussing a business deal when Beau warned, "You'd better not screw around with us, because look what happened to Aaron Iturra."

Mary, who'd been listening in the next room, came in and added, "And they'll never convict me because my homies will protect me."

Another time, Mary said to Larry "Truth" Martin, "Beau would be proud of me because of what happened to Aaron." All through this period, the gang were plotting their crimes, discussing them on the phone, and still the police could not touch them. They began to feel a sense of invulnerability, of impunity.

Most, if not all, of the gang members were dropouts, ne'er-do-wells. They wouldn't get up until late morning and they would plan their activities for one, two, three o'clock in the morning. They'd be out all night, high on drugs, committing crimes.

The gang had become their reason for being, the gang had become the entity they owed their allegiance to, the gang had become their mother and father and lover. They felt the power and respect that gang membership gave them and vowed not to give it up.

The boy watched from the banks of the river as the police divers dressed in black, form-fitting scuba gear walked into the water and disappeared below the surface. They seemed to be looking for something, but since he had been raised by his father not to interfere in someone else's affairs, he kept fishing and minded his own business. Besides, getting supper was more important than anything the cops were doing.

The boy was fishing off the banks of the river a hundred yards down from where the cops were. It had been a quiet morning, with no bites, when he heard one of the cops spring out from the water and yell, "I found them!"

What the cop had found were the bullets that Brown had thrown into the river. Despite that exciting find, which would help the forensics of the case considerably, there was still no gun.

A few minutes later, the boy felt something tugging on his line. "I got something!" he said out loud to no one in particular. He began reeling it in, and felt the strong tug continue on the line. *Boy, it's a big one*, he thought. And it was.

A .38 caliber Smith and Wesson revolver with four-inch barrel and a brown handle that Eugene forensic specialists would later identify as the gun Jim Elstad had used to murder Aaron Iturra.

FRIDAY, OCTOBER 7, 1994

It was a perfect fall day at Lane Memorial Cemetery, brisk, sunny, full of tears at the graveside. Aaron Iturra lay in his open coffin, wearing the new clothes his sister Tina had picked out for the occasion.

On his chest were three tribal eagle feathers, symbolizing maturity, wisdom and strength. Mourners walked by, dropping in remembrances, looking at the pristine visage of a teenage boy cut down in his prime. Holding her baby, Angel Elstad walked by and remembered a conversation not too long before over at Mary's.

"I want Aaron killed," Mary had said.

Angel was struck by her matter-of-fact tone. "Aaron sent Beau back to MacLaren and he has to pay for it." At first, the gang members didn't know whether to take Mary seriously. But Angel knew it was real that night she heard the shot, when Jim came back to their house afterwards, and then walked over to Mary's to tell her he had done as she'd asked.

When Cameron Slade looked at Aaron's lifeless face, he thought about the times the gang would be meeting and talking about Aaron and Beau and it would be Mary who would bring up capping Aaron and the rest of them would say they would do it.

Linda Miller remembered seeing Mary with a gun and, during the time Mary had it in her possession, hearing her say "This is the gun that's going to take care of the problem." To Linda, Cameron and Angel, it was clear exactly what she meant.

Another time at Mary's house, Linda saw a list of five names printed on plain white paper. When she asked Mary who was on the list, Mary said, "These are the ones who 'dissed' Beau and they are going to be killed." Aaron's was the first name on the list.

Watching as Aaron's coffin was closed and lowered into his grave, Janyce's tear-filled eyes looked up long enough to scan the crowd. No matter how hard she looked, she could not find Mary Thompson. She just couldn't figure it out. Mary had been Aaron's friend, his confidante, and now, today, when he needed her most, she had deserted him. One of the last times Aaron had talked about Mary, he had been visibly upset.

"Mom, it's really scary over there, 'cause Mary is gaining control and power over these kids," Aaron had told her.

"Have you discussed this with her?"

"No. She keeps yelling at me for not taking care of Beau. She called me a liar. She said I was trying to get Beau into trouble by saying that he was running around with the same old gang kids."

"I can't understand—"

"What can I say? What can I *do*?" Aaron shouted, throwing his hands up in disgust.

"You're not responsible, Aaron," Janyce answered.

Janyce knew from what Aaron had told her, and from her daughter Tina, who had visited Mary once or twice, that Mary Thompson was a generous woman. She opened her house to troubled kids, some of whom had no place to live. But the turnaround almost seemed like, like . . . *they owed her*. For her putting herself out for them, they owed her. It was bizarre, Janyce thought.

She turned back to the grave.

A Baptist minister gave the final benedictions. "Ashes to ashes, dust to dust . . ." The minister's voice trailed off and in Janyce's mind, it was two weeks before Aaron's death. Aaron was in the kitchen, where the phone was, and he picked it up on the first ring. Janyce was in the living room, reading the paper.

"Yeah, hi, Mary," said Aaron, clearly not pleased that she was calling.

He listened for a moment and then said, "Well, whatever!"

More silence, then, "Do what you gotta do, whatever! I'm gonna do what I gotta do!"

Janyce recalled that he was screaming at Mary, because she was giving him a hard time about testifying against Beau. Finally, he shouted, "Do whatever ya gotta do" again and hung up.

Then she remembered the Sunday night of Aaron's death. He had come home late that afternoon and was sitting in the kitchen with Tina while Janyce prepared dinner. After dinner, homemade spaghetti and meat sauce, they went out into the living room to relax.

"Hey, Mom, you'll never believe this."

"What?" said Janyce.

"Wayde Hudson and Jim Elstad are gonna take the big guy down."

"Who's 'the big guy'?" Janyce asked, puzzled.

"Well, I am," said Aaron. "They were bragging about what they were gonna do to some guys at school. Cameron Slade and Larry Martin."

"You mean 'Mr. Preppie' is gonna get ya?" said Janyce, laughing and referring to Elstad by the nickname she had given him. "There's no way those two kids are gonna beat you up."

Aaron stopped and thought about that for a moment and then answered, "I may be big and I may be strong, but a knife and a bullet can take me down in a minute."

And then they kind of laughed about it. Why not? *It just never entered my mind that anything like this would really happen*, Janyce thought, *and I don't think it entered Aaron's mind either.*

Looking up, she saw her husband. He was the father of the surviving children, a man who had left Janyce and his kids. He comes for the funeral only, looking like the grieving father who had been part of Aaron's life. *What a phony*, Janyce thought. One of her kids whispered to her before they got to the cemetery, "Mom, Dad never cared that much when Aaron was alive!"

As the minister finished his prayers, Jim Michaud carefully watched each and every mourner as the crowd melted away to their cars. He, too, was looking for Mary, and yet, she was nowhere to be found.

Justice has a way of being lenient, even in the case of murderers. Especially murderers. And though Assistant District Attorney Steve Skelton could probably have made a case against Jim Elstad and Joe Brown for premeditated murder, there really was no point.

Skelton knew that even if he got a conviction, they would never be executed. The United States might have an imperfect legal system, but one thing it didn't do was condemn kids to the death chamber, regardless of their crimes.

Most death penalty cases take years before the appeals are exhausted and cost the taxpayers millions of dollars. It cost less to imprison someone for life. In the case of Elstad and Brown, Skelton carefully evaluated the evidence and decided it was not a murder one case. After a quick plea bargain agreement with the boys' attorneys, a deal was reached: they would each plead to lesser murder charges and be sentenced accordingly.

It was early November and a chill was in the air. The Pacific Northwest has moderate temperatures all year round, but when November comes, things seem to get particularly colder, the rain wetter, the sunlight more diffuse.

On November 7, 1994, Joe Brown entered a guilty plea to murder in the second degree. Four days later, on November 11, Elstad also entered a plea of guilty to the crime of murder two. They would be sentenced on separate dates.

DECEMBER 6, 1994

It was 8:30 in the morning, time for Joe Brown to get his judgment. But before he did, Oregon law, like that of many states, allowed the victim's family to address the court before sentencing. And Janyce Iturra had a lot to say to the boy who had participated in her son's murder.

"Would you give for the court record your name, please?" asked Marion Johnston, the court reporter.

"Janyce Iturra. I'd like to step around so Joe can at least look me in the face." Janyce stepped from behind the lectern she had been placed at off to the side, to a space directly in front of Joe Brown. He looked up briefly, then back down at his hands in his lap. Judge Kip Leonard leaned forward from the bench, anxious to hear what Janyce had to say.

"First of all, I want you to hear my pain and to let you know what you've taken away from us. I'd like to know what made you think you had the right to play God and to determine whether somebody lived or died."

She waited before continuing. Joe Brown did not answer.

"Aaron was your friend and you didn't stop it. As far as I'm concerned, you might as well have pulled the trigger yourself because you didn't take the chance you had to stop it."

It was her turn to open up with both barrels, with words instead of bullets, words that would place the condemned boy's crime in proper context.

"The losses that we have felt since this has happened is that two of my children here didn't feel like coming because they didn't think it would make a difference. See, you took their big brother away. You took their protector. You took my first-born child away. He was the man of our house and he's been there since the age of nine filling that role. I have never felt fear in this town until you took my son away while he was sleeping in the security of my home. *You understand that?* It's a very cold, violent way to take somebody's life."

Janyce paused, looking down at her notes, then up again, struggling with her emotions.

"You get to live ten years in the state pen with three meals a day and television and a good time. We live a life of nothing now. We have memories and I have worn his coat since the day I got it back. This is all I have to hold on to and I want you to know that. This is all I have to hold on to. On Thanksgiving, we had to visit a grave. Do you understand that?"

Suddenly, Joe looked up and replied, "Yes, I do."

"You have all the rights. You are protected and we're not. I have all the financial burden and you do not. I have four kids to take care of at home. You don't. You don't know what it's like to hear the kids cry in the middle of the night and tell me how cheated they are and how unfair this thing is . . ."

Her voice trailed off. Joe Brown looked up again and Janyce fixed him with a stare that pinned him frozen.

The view of the garage as the killers approached the house.
(*Eugene Department of Public Safety*)

The bloodstained mattress on which Aaron Iturra was found
mortally wounded. (*Eugene Department of Public Safety*)

Aaron Iturra posing in his bedroom
where he would later be shot.
(*Janyce Iturra*)

Another view of the makeshift bedroom at the back of the garage - a typical teenager's cluttered room where a murder would soon be committed. (*Eugene Department of Public Safety*)

Blood spattered on the beer bottle upon impact of the shot that eventually killed Aaron Iturra.

(*Eugene Department of Public Safety*)

The living room window on the right was the one Joe Brown tapped on to make sure everyone was asleep before the killers entered the house. (*Eugene Department of Public Safety*)

The garage entrance through which the killers skulked on their way to Aaron's bedroom. (*Eugene Department of Public Safety*)

Inspection of the murder scene by forensic specialists. (*Eugene Department of Public Safety*)

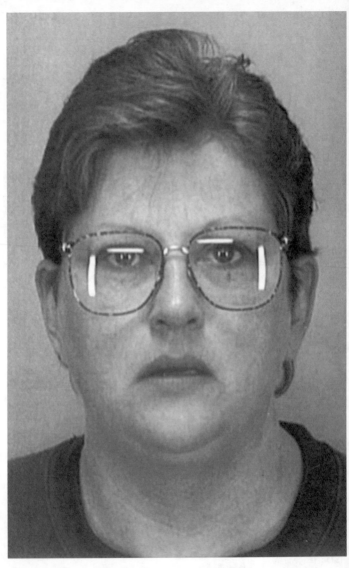

A mug shot of convicted murderer "Gang Mom" herself, Mary Louise Thompson. (*Eugene Department of Public Safety*)

Joe Brown, the point man, who re-enacted Aaron's murder for Michaud and the police.
(*Eugene Department of Public Safety*)

Preppy-looking Jim Elstad, the man who pulled the trigger and killed Aaron Iturra.
(*Eugene Department of Public Safety*)

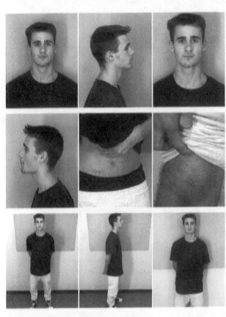

Police recorded Jim Elstad's pristine appearance so that he would not be able to claim later that the police abused him during questioning. (*Eugene Department of Public Safety*)

An unidentified man stands at the spot in the river where Joe Brown threw the murder weapon and bullets.

(*Eugene Department of Public Safety*)

Beau Flynn, Mary Thompson's son, who led police on a wild chase across the city of Eugene until he was finally captured.
(*Eugene Department of Public Safety*)

Jim Michaud, the detective who broke the "Gang Mom" case and brought Mary Thompson to the bar of justice. (*Eugene Department of Public Safety*)

Carrie, Aaron's girlfriend, was next to him in the bed when he was shot. *(Janyce Iturra)*

Janyce always felt that Aaron was the family's protector, as reflected by the epitaph on his gravestone. *(Janyce Iturra)*

Aaron Benjamin Joseph Iturra

Born: December 23, 1975
Life Taken: October 3, 1994

PROTECTOR

SON • BROTHER

TOO WELL LOVED TO BE FORGOTTEN

"Who gave you the right to kill him?"

You could have heard a pin drop in the courtroom.

"Who gave you the right to kill him? If I were the judge sitting there I would make sure that you were sentenced to death. I feel that the only justice is that you don't breathe again. But the law does not allow you to face the death chamber. The judge will give you time, but I sentence you to something else."

She stood straighter and intoned the words like she was his judge and jury.

"Joe Brown, I sentence you to have to think of Aaron Iturra's face while he lay sleeping before you let him be shot. I sentence you to take long, slow breaths, breaths you stole from him. I sentence you to remember those words, because that's what you deserve.

"So my idea of you, Joe Brown, is that you are nothing. You are absolutely nothing, and the sad thing is that you are alive here today and he's not. You had seven minutes to walk down to my house at one thirty in the morning and you could have done something. I hope you have a life of hell because that's what you have put us through."

Janyce looked up at the court, muttered a perfunctory "Thank you," and sat down. The judge then sentenced Brown to ten years in prison.

That night, Janyce's appearance at Brown's sentencing was all over the local news. A few people called to give support, because while she had been calm and collected in court, she had been upset afterwards, reacting to the delayed stress of talking in detail about Aaron's death. Janyce was in the middle of preparing dinner when there was a knock at the door.

"Oh, my God, Mary!"

It was Mary Thompson all right, with a big smile on her face. She busted right in like "Ed Norton" visiting "Ralph Kramden." Janyce was shocked speechless for a second until her tongue untied.

"Mary, you have your nerve—"

Mary wouldn't let her finish.

"Oh, Janyce, I'm *so* sorry for what happened to Aaron."

"Mary, I tried you so many times and you never called back."

"Oh, I was having problems with, you know, my beeper and my phone and then my dog Lars died."

"Look, Mary, I . . ."

"Oh, I'm so sorry for Aaron being killed. And you know, I was still angry for Aaron having betrayed me."

"*Betrayed you*, Mary . . ." Janyce began in indignation, only to be cut off again.

"I am so sorry for having Aaron killed, and if he hadn't betrayed me . . ."

"Mary—"

"I'm so sorry for having to have it happen."

"You didn't even show up at the funeral!" Janyce yelled.

"The officers, the officers, they said I shouldn't go," she said in a flurry of words.

Janyce didn't want to hear any of that crap. Mary had deserted her friend and his family on the day of his funeral. What kind of person did that? You could look for hidden meanings but the most obvious was that Mary just didn't care.

Then suddenly, the whole tone of the conversation switched.

"Well, Jan," said Mary rationally, "I just really want to be your friend. Why don't we just do coffee? Call me."

"I don't think so right now. No, I don't want to be your friend right now."

Mary left. Angry and hurt, Janyce slammed the door behind her. Janyce stood there and fumed. The nerve of that woman, coming here when Aaron . . .

"Oh, my God!"

Had Mary just said, "I am so sorry for having Aaron killed"? No, wait a sec, that can't be.

All night, and into the following morning, Janyce questioned what she had heard. And if she had heard what she thought she had, what should she do? By morning she had decided. She went down to police headquarters to the Violent Crimes Squad.

"Jim," she began, and told Michaud of her conversation the previous night with Mary.

Michaud was surprised that Mary had slipped up, but in eighteen years as a cop he had seen other con men make crucial mistakes that brought them down. He had recently worked a case of a major jewel thief and con man named *Thomas Moran*, who had operated up and down the I–5 corridor, who thought he could continue getting away with his crimes, until Michaud got on his trail and, like a bloodhound, wouldn't get off it till Moran began to make mistakes. Michaud was there all right, ready to pounce.

Maybe that was going on here. Maybe the pressure was finally getting to Mary.

"Are you sure about what Mary said?" Michaud asked.

"I heard what I heard. Yes, I'm sure," Janyce answered.

"All right, Janyce, look . . ." Michaud grabbed both her hands and stared into her eyes. "I need to tell you, this woman is more involved than you or I can ever imagine. Now, no more talking to her. Do not put yourself out there for her and definitely do not meet her for coffee. Oh, and one more thing."

"What?"

"I'm going to get her."

DECEMBER 19, 1994

Janyce Iturra looked at the space that used to be her son Aaron's bedroom. When she and the kids moved back in, she'd cleaned up. Gone were the blood-stains and the bloody mattress. When you looked around, it seemed like he'd be home any minute. But of course, that was just a fantasy. She turned, went out into the garage and got into her car.

As she drove, she thought she should be at work. Janyce still worked the early morning shift at the department store. Her employer had been nice enough to give her the time off for the court proceedings she needed to attend.

By the time she reached downtown, her mind had turned to the place it felt most comfortable with lately: revenge. Revenge was on Janyce's mind when she entered court for Jim Elstad's sentencing. Sure, revenge wouldn't put food in her children's mouths, nor would it bring Aaron back. But it felt *good*.

"Mrs. Iturra, this is your opportunity to make a statement, and if you would like to come up and sit in the chair next to Mr. Skelton, please feel free," began court reporter Hugh Wheeler.

Steve Skelton looked up from his seat at the prosecutor's table as Janyce walked around it and sat down next to him. Janyce looked down at her notes, shuffled them in her hand, then looked up.

Janyce made her statement coldly and methodically, reviewing the way the murder of her son had been carried out. Years from now, when the parole board reviewed the file to make a decision about whether or not Jim Elstad got out on parole, she wanted to be sure they knew what a cold-hearted son-of-a-bitch he really was.

"I would like you to look at his senior picture," Janyce said to Jim Elstad. She extended it to Elstad, and Wheeler, the court reporter, came over and took it. Then he handed it to Elstad, who gazed at it.

"I just got it a couple days after he died. That was *your* friend, and you held his life in your hand just like you're holding his picture now. You had choices. He was a human being, and in that seven minutes that it took you to go from your house to my home, you committed the most cruelest crime on Aaron, on me and my family, *your friend.*

"What you robbed my three girls of, and my surviving son of, was an uncle for their children, a best man at their wedding, a companion in old age. You robbed me of grandchildren."

Then she described how she came to discover his injured body, and holding him in her arms. "There was blood everywhere. Too much. There was brain matter there. I did not know what it was until later. And I still knew my son was going to make it because he was the strongest person I knew."

She talked about how it took a while to find out that he had been shot in the head and the embarrassment she and her kids went through when, "We were made prisoners in our own home. We were checked for gunpowder residue on our hands. We couldn't leave.

"Do you know how long I had to wait before I could leave and see my son? Eight thirty. Seven hours after you shot him. I lost seven hours with my son, seven of his last hours on earth, because *you* shot him. *You!* I finally got down there and you know how many hours I had left? Two. He died at ten thirty, Jim. From what I understand, it was at the same time your sister was having her baby. Congratulations on being an uncle," she said sarcastically.

Janyce paused and took a drink out of a paper cup of water, then continued.

"The first time I got to kiss him was at the funeral. A little late, don't you think?"

Elstad didn't answer, just stared at her. What was there to say? No psychological evaluation had been done on him, but from the description of the way he committed the crime and his lack of guilt afterwards, and even as Janyce poured her heart out, it sounded like he was probably a psychopath.

Elstad didn't feel guilt. He just did what made him feel good. Like shooting a defenseless teenager in the back of his head as he slept.

"It's going to be ten years, fifteen years before you see your little niece. But it will be a lifetime before my kids ever see their brother. It will be when they're passing. And the one thing that I'm going to sentence you to is that every night you go to sleep, the last thing you see, is my son sleeping before you shot him. And that every breath you breathe is a breath you took from him. And you remember that for the rest of your miserable life, because I can't give you any worse sentence than *that*."

She sat down and the judge sentenced Jim Elstad to fifteen years behind bars. The guards led him away into the bowels of the prison system, away from his family, away from society. Maybe he'd turn his life around in prison. Maybe he'd get an education there. Maybe he'd realize the horror of what he had done and begin to feel.

Like the "bad guys" on "NYPD Blue." *Not*!

Michaud had been watching from the back of the courtroom. *Good*, he thought. *One less murderer to worry about. And now he's gone. Two down and one to go. The one who set the whole thing up and continues to walk free.*

Mary Thompson.

THREE

The Wire

TEN

MARY WAS BORN NOVEMBER 23, 1954, in Massillon, Ohio. Her mother, Ethyl Fockler, was a nurse with three children. Her brothers at the time of her birth were twelve and seventeen, while her sister was sixteen. Mary's, though, wasn't a planned birth. In fact, Ethyl figured she was too old to have any more kids. She was wrong.

Marriage and family therapists today quickly pinpoint where family dynamics go wrong and a child follows the wrong path. A child brought into the world unplanned may get the message that her birth was a burden to her family and as a consequence, begin to act out. In Mary's case, it is hard to tell what she learned subliminally. While her father, a steelworker in one of the local mills, loved her dearly, her sister would later recall that as she matured, Mary became a bully, acting out with tantrums and violence.

"Yeah, I was pretty spoiled," Mary Thompson recalled during an interview in 1996. "Judy [her sister] couldn't handle that. None of them could. I remember one time the ice cream truck came around and my dad said, 'What kind do you want?' and I said, 'Cherry, raspberry, banana,' several flavors, and he got them all for me.

"Then my brother Joel said, 'Can I have a bit of one of those?' And I went 'Noooooooooooo!' " Mary continued, sounding like Red Skelton's greedy character "The Mean Widdle Kid."

Her other brother Bobby was more into Italian food than ice cream. Sometime in 1967, Bobby was driven by his brother Joel to the pizza place where his wife worked. Bobby walked in, pulled a gun and shot his wife dead. Sentenced to prison, by the summer of 1968 he was serving his time in the Ohio Correctional Facility when inmates started a riot. Watching the riot coverage on TV at home, his father became alarmed. Would his son be safe? The old man worried so much for his son's safety that he had a heart attack.

"All I know was that dad was on the floor, and I just wanted everybody to shut up and just deal with it," instead of the confusion which reigned, Mary recalled. When her father died a month later, it was as much from a broken heart as anything else. He was the parent of one murderer, with another still to come.

Heart attacks, murder, chaos, confusion. It was more than enough to cope with. Joel, though, couldn't cope and a month after his dad died, he tried to take his own life by shooting himself in the chest with a rifle. It was, apparently, his way of coping with the shame of having driven Bobby to his rendezvous with murder.

Unfortunately, Joel was rather ineffectual as a suicide. Not only did he fail to kill himself, the bullet hit his spinal cord and paralyzed him from the waist down.

"Before Joel came back home, they put him in a rehabilitation hospital in Cleveland," Mary recalls. "On Saturday, we'd go visit Joel at the hospital and on Sunday, we'd go visit Bobby at the pen. That's pretty functional, isn't it?"

If you want to tell a lie, the way to get it over is by including some truth to it. Likewise, if you want to explain inexplicable actions, like murder, take some responsibility and then lay on the soft stuff. It was a lesson Mary would use time and again to manipulate those around her.

"My mother was a wonderful person. There wasn't anything in the world she couldn't do for you. There wasn't anything she wouldn't do for Mary," her sister Judy recalls. And yet Mary, who as a child was a cute flower girl at Judy's wedding, thought of her mother as "a neurotic idiot." As for Judy, Mary hated her because of her conventional lifestyle: happy marriage, successful business and three kids. Everything Mary didn't, and perhaps couldn't, have because of her emotional make-up.

Mary had so charmed her mother into believing that her youngest daughter was a wonderful human being and credit to the human race that the hard-working Ethyl bought her a brand new sports car, a Volkswagen Karmann Ghia, for one of her birthdays. How's that for spoiling your kid? But gradually, as she got older, Mary Fockler's true personality as a liar and a cheat came out.

She managed to convince her mother to let her use her credit cards before the poor woman went into the operating room for surgery. Her sister maintains that Mary, on numerous occasions, wrote bad checks on Ethyl's account. Judy even had to close off her mom's home to Mary because Mary had been stealing the furniture!

After adolescence, Mary Fockler made attempts to go straight, attending various colleges, but every time, she would drop out. She began hanging out with the wrong type of crowd, amoral bikers and other types of degenerates. Recognizing the seriousness of her sister's problems, Judy pleaded with Mary to get counseling. Why not go to a psychiatrist who could help her? Mary demurred but eventually she was forced to see one; Mary tried to kill herself by cutting her wrists and in the aftermath, Judy committed her to a psychiatric hospital for a short stay that was interrupted when Mary got a Legal Aid lawyer to get her out of the "loony bin."

Mary Fockler had failed at everything she had attempted: school, familial relations, the basic adjustments and socialization that every child goes through on the way to maturity. Figuring life might be better in the military, Mary enlisted in the Women's Army Corps and became a WAC.

Wacky was more like it. Mary couldn't adjust to the Army any more than she could to civilian life. Eventually, she was given a psychological discharge.

After surviving two strokes, Ethyl died on February 14, 1976. Some said Mary's behavior drove her to her grave. Ethyl had always liked to see Mary in dresses, but for the funeral, Mary showed up wearing jeans and a denim jacket. It was her way of showing respect.

Soon after the funeral, her gang career with the Hells Angels began.

Throughout the next few months following the trials, Ric Raynor, the gang cop, continued to speak sporadically with Mary Thompson. He still felt that she had been lured into the gang lifestyle and had not intended to become a gangster.

Within the Eugene Police Department, Raynor was not the only one who ascribed to this theory. The police chief himself felt Mary was not the monster that Michaud believed her to be. Even Beau Flynn's former parole officer had an opinion counter to Michaud's.

Virginia Newby was an Oregon Youth Authority parole officer who was assigned to fourteen-year-old Beau Flynn's case back in 1992. At that time, he was committed to the MacLaren Youth Correctional Facility. She recalled Beau claiming to be a "Crip." Newby felt that his behavior revealed ". . . his fascination with guns, the weapons that escalated him from a punk kid to a dangerous felon."

Newby remembered Mary as a very distraught mother, who "desperately wanted her only son to show her respect." Beau repaid his mother's love by betraying her authority. "He had stolen from her and created all sorts of havoc." How ironic; Beau was just following family tradition, though Newby did not know that.

As for Mary, she felt that her authority had been completely undermined because Beau had become a ward of the state. All she was left with was a photo album full of childhood memories, and a growing sense of guilt.

Newby theorized that "by going public with her story, [it] allowed her to shift the blame for her son's behavior from her own failures as a mother to the alleged influence of the notorious gangs. No doubt it was a tremendous boost to her ego to be showered with attention as well."

Mary's sounding the alarm that "Next, it could be your kid" was her way of focusing attention on herself as a "good mom" wishing to save others from a similar situation.

"In my opinion, her interest did not lie in protecting the community or in saving gang-affected youth," Newby added. "Instead, I believe Thompson wanted desperately to be seen as a victim of circumstance, a knowledgeable, caring parent in a crusade to save her son."

Michaud didn't buy any of it. Mary Thompson was a con woman, first and foremost. Her past showed that, and if he was able to prove that she had put that "contract" out on Aaron, she was going down for a hard fall. But anyone who thought killing Aaron was just a means to save her son was being short-sighted. There were bigger things at stake here.

Frustrated at getting nowhere, Michaud sat at his desk, went out into the field, used all of his resources to try and get conclusive evidence to nail Mary for setting up the Iturra murder. And he was failing. The case was cold, threatening to leap into the "double-wrapped freezer " pile on his desk unless he did something. But what? The practical aspects of the case threatened to shut it down.

Any police investigation over a period of time takes up man-hours. It costs money. And the Thompson case, with Michaud spearheading the investigation, was costing too much in regular man-hours and overtime. Prosecutor Steve Skelton periodically consulted with Michaud, and when he saw a lack of progress in the case, decided to punt.

"Let's offer Mary a deal. She can plead guilty to a

single count of hindering prosecution." At least they'd get her for something and with a sympathetic judge and a little luck, some jail time.

Michaud was reluctant to make a deal. He knew the woman was a killer and didn't want to let her get away with murder. But what was he to do? Besides, it wasn't his choice. He didn't prosecute; the state did.

There are two types of assistant district attorneys. One is the young buck, looking to make a name for himself and then take his reputation and go into private practice where he can make big money. The second is the career civil servant, the nameless, faceless sword of justice, the guy who quietly prosecutes felons year after year with little or no fanfare and gets his kicks from the satisfaction of getting scuzbuckets off the street. Steve Skelton, with twenty-two years in the d.a.'s office, fell into the latter category.

Middle-aged and graying, you wouldn't give him a second look on the street. He didn't wear Armani or Versace, just rumpled prosecutor gray. But behind his desk in the plain office where he receives visitors, he looks like a dynamic, implacable foe of evil.

It was Skelton who reviewed all the evidence in the "Gang Mom" case that Michaud brought him, and made the decision when to prosecute. And it was Skelton who now summoned Mary Thompson to the district attorney's office.

We don't indict people because they have killed somebody, we indict them because we can prove they have killed somebody, Skelton thought. In Mary Thompson's case, proving murder was just too damn difficult.

When Mary arrived, she took a seat directly in front

of Skelton. Off to the side, Michaud silently slouched in his seat. Skelton rose up from behind his desk and offered Mary the deal: Plead to hindering prosecution, the police drop their investigation and it's all over. Minimum jail time would follow, and then release. If Mary was indeed guilty, it was perfect. She'd be back with her family in no time.

"No," answered Mary firmly.

Michaud sat up. This was getting interesting.

"No?" Skelton asked in a disbelieving tone. Michaud, meanwhile, felt elated. It isn't too often in police work that you get a second crack.

"I didn't do anything wrong. Why should I plead to something I didn't do?"

"Absolutely, Mary, why should you?" Michaud drawled.

For a moment, the two looked at each other. It was cat and mouse now. Neither was going to give ground. And it was personal, between *them*.

After Mary left, Michaud called his bosses and told them that Mary had rejected the deal. The case was still active. Michaud also knew something else of particular relevance.

Mary was sure that no matter what Michaud did, he wouldn't catch her. That, he realized, made her vulnerable. Mary liked to brag to the media. Might she not do the same in the privacy of her home?

To get her, he needed somebody inside her home. An undercover operative was out of the question. What was he supposed to do, get Johnny Depp? "21 Jump Street" was a TV show; in reality, few cops could pose as minors and get away with it. Besides, Mary kept a pretty close circle of kids around her. Anyone new would surely raise suspicions.

That left only one avenue of investigation that would let them eavesdrop on what was going on inside the house. They needed to monitor Mary's conversations with the gang members. If his theory of the crime was right, it should yield the true reason for Aaron's death.

IN THE CIRCUIT COURT OF THE STATE OF
OREGON FOR LANE COUNTY

IN THE MATTER OF AN APPLICATION FOR)
AN EX PARTE ORDER AUTHORIZING)
INTERCEPTION OF WIRE AND/OR CELLULAR)
COMMUNICATION OF MARY LOUISE THOMPSON)

AFFIDAVIT

STATE OF OREGON)
)ss
County of Lane)

I, James Michaud, being duly sworn on oath, hereby depose and say:

I am a police officer with the Eugene Police Department and have been so employed for the past 18 years. I am currently assigned as a detective in the Violent Crimes Detail in the Investigative Unit. I have received extensive formal training in homicide investigations and my experience is based on the investigation of hundreds of cases involving violent crimes against persons including homicide.

This affidavit is submitted in support of an application by Lane County District Attorney, F. Douglas Harcieroad, for an order authorizing the interception of telephonic communications by Mary Louise Thompson occurring at 442 Waite Street, Eugene, Lane 2C County Oregon, over hard-wired telephone number (503) 555-6023 and any and all conversations by Mary Louise Thompson on cellular telephone number (503) 555-1505. I have been assigned as the case agent investigating the criminal homicide of Aaron Benjamin Iturra. As a result of my personal participation in this investigation, through interviews with witnesses and by analysis of reports submitted by other officers of the Eugene Police Department and discussions with the Lane County Medical Examiner, Dr. Samuel Vickers, I am familiar with all aspects of this investigation.

Affidavit of Detective James Michaud

Wiretaps have gotten a bum reputation ever since 1972 when Nixon bugged Democratic National Headquarters. In subsequent criminal investigations, local and federal officials violated people's civil rights in the indiscriminate use of bugging.

But starting with the 1980's, tapping a suspected criminal's phone became the latest high-tech tool in law enforcement to yield results. For instance, the federal government was able to bug John Gotti's headquarters, so successfully, in fact, that the evidence gathered from the bug led to Gotti's eventual conviction.

In the state of Oregon, an officer can only get a bug or tap by showing the judge conclusively, in the form of an affidavit, that all reasonable investigative avenues have been exhausted, and that the only way to gather evidence against a suspected felon, Mary Thompson in this case, was to eavesdrop on her phone conversations.

The judge saw things Michaud's way and granted the order.

In the old days, a police officer would actually have to steal his way into the suspect's home when he was away and physically plant a listening device inside the phone. Today, because of advances in telephonic technology, police can establish their tap right from the source—the phone company.

Michaud walked over and showed them his court order granting permission to tap Mary's line. The phone company was extremely cooperative in throwing the switches that would allow police to listen in on the phone conversations to and from Mary Thompson's house without being detected.

With the wiring in place, the next step was establishing where the bug would be manned, and who would man it. Violent Crimes had had enough experience with tapping on previous cases to know that setting up a listening post at police headquarters would not work. It was too cramped as it was, and the last thing Michaud wanted was some stupid rookie to mess things up by throwing the wrong switch. No, better to work off-premises.

A secret listening post was established in an office

building in downtown Eugene. An office was rented for the month—it was not anticipated the tap would go further—chairs were brought in, Marantz tape recorders, phones and head phones were set up on plain wooden tables. The phone company electronically tied Mary's phone in with the one at the listening post. When hers rang, the listening post's did too and the DNR did the rest.

DNR stands for "Dial Number Recorder." It is a unit that automatically monitors all incoming and outgoing calls, carefully recording the date and time of the call, as well as the internal catalogue number. Like the retail "Caller ID" available to consumers, the DNR registers the name of the incoming caller and the number they're calling from. But the human factor, the people manning the phones, are just as important, if not more so.

The government will not let any police department monitor all calls. They have to be relevant to the case, as set out in the affidavit. Therefore, any court order to wiretap comes with minimization instructions, which require the officer manning the tap not to listen in during certain types of calls. Generally, calls involving husband and wife, spiritual counselors and lawyers are minimized and that was the case with the Thompson wiretap.

Assistant D.A. Steve Skelton initiated discussions with Michaud and the administration people from the Eugene Police Department about when the wire could be broken. Since it was an aggravated murder investigation, maintaining the wiretap would be given as high a priority as possible.

A consensus was reached that the wiretaps would not be broken to foil a crime against property, for instance grand theft auto. They might attempt to thwart such a crime, but they wouldn't shut down the wiretap for the purpose of going out and stopping a crime against property.

The wire would only be *burned* [compromised] where there was a chance the gang would physically hurt someone. They would take the chance that Mary Thompson would not realize that the police's principal source of information would be a phone tap.

With the wire's protocol set, and the wiring itself in place, it was time to begin. Manning the headphones were Michaud and Rainey. Ric Raynor, though, was conspicuously absent. He had been taken off the case, which made him feel slighted and, at least to one reporter who interviewed him, bitter. But the case was bigger than any one cop's feelings. Murder always is.

ELEVEN

AT 11:17 P.M. ON Friday, January 13, 1995, the DNR turned on. Michaud was on duty and he picked up the earphones. It was a call from Lisa Fentress for Beau Flynn.

"Hello?" Beau answered.

"Hi," said Lisa.

"This is his night."

"Yep."

"He came down to visit me, homes. He didn't bring his real car. He stole one."

"Did you say he's driving a stolen car?"

"Ha ha, yeah. But he changed the plates and the VIN number so if he got pulled over they couldn't say nothing to him."

As the conversation proceeded it became clear that "he" was a business associate of Beau's from Portland who trafficked in stolen cars. It was clear that Beau had an intimate knowledge of the business.

"I gotta page my home boy and see what's going on," Beau continued.

"All right."

" 'Cause I think he already has a hotel. I think he might be talking to Nina."

"*Nina Jones?*"

"No! That bitch got my dope, man! She gave me the fake shit, homes! She gave me fake stuff, you know that? She switched it! I'm gonna kill that girl!"

"How do you know it was fake?"

"I f---ing tested it tonight. She gave me a fat rock of the real stuff, but the rest of it, we were bouncing it off the damn floor!"

Well, that's one drug deal Beau won't make, Michaud thought.

Later in the day, at 2:01 p.m., Beau placed a call to gang member *Tom Simmons*.

"Hey, what's up, homes?"

"What's up?" Tom answered.

"So what's up for tonight?"

"I don't know. Let's hook up," Tom suggested.

"All right, homes, because I want to f---in' steal that car. If we could take that out and strip it for a grip . . ."

"Yeah," Tom agreed.

" 'Cause there's this chop shop dealer up in Portland."

"Oh, yeah?"

"Yeah. We could drive them up there and sell their butt. Each one of 'em. And the guy don't take f---ed up cars. He takes like Cadillacs and s--- like that."

"Yeah, I know."

"And he'll pay us like four hundred for each car."

"Cool."

"So we could drive like four cars up a night."

"Ha ha ha!"

"And then after we steal 'em, we can park 'em and throw tarps on 'em."

"Okay."

Beau had apparently had such a tough day planning out his criminal activities that he had to take a nap. His next phone call wasn't until 10:53 p.m.

"Hello?" his friend Sam Warthan began.

"What's up?" Beau answered.

"Hey."

"Yeah, she said that, uh, any time before one o'clock and then she knows where a house is too."

They're planning a burglary, Michaud thought.

"Okay. I just called you to say it would probably be longer 'cause my clothes ain't done drying."

"Yeah, but she has it. She's ready."

"Okay."

"And then," Beau continued, "we could drive her up there probably and out where that thing exactly is at."

"Well, I got a house over here."

"Oh, yeah, we got a couple there then?"

"Yeah."

So it would be a few burglaries.

"All right. Cool then."

"But I can't do this one house."

"Why?"

"Because I've already done it and the neighbors know me."

Michaud chuckled and said to Rainey, "At least he's got some common sense."

"What's that mean?" Beau asked.

"On the other hand, Beau does tend to be a bit dense," Michaud added as Sam explained, "They know me. They know what I look like."

"Oh. So you want to do something else then?"

"No, I would, you all could do it."

"Well, damn."

"There's four guaranteed straps in there."

The cops stiffened.

"Huh?"

"There's four guaranteed straps in there," Sam repeated.

Both Michaud and Rainey knew that *straps* was gang slang for guns.

"Well, I don't understand. Where's Tom at?"

"He's in the shower."

"All right. Is Tom gonna do it with me?"

"Probably."

"All right. That'd be cool then. I ain't gonna do it by myself necessarily."

"Well, I'll probably even go in."

"Neh neh neh, yeah, but we'll have a strap, we'll be strapped for now. You know. Strapped. I'll go pick up some bullets today, later on."

"Which one you getting? That twenty-two?"

"Yeah."

"A revolver?"

"Yep. They still bust cars, though. You know?"

"Yeah. Where's your f---in' nine at?"

"Dude, that's a forty-five," Beau corrected. "I can't find it. Ha ha. I left it at the broad's house, man. But no, I think I know where it's at. 'Cause I can't go over there 'cause she's on vacation with her parents."

"Let's just go rob her house," Sam answered.

"Yeah, right. I can't do that, homes. That ain't cool like that. The girl don't even know it's there, though."

"Oh."

"I haven't seen it."

"Oh, well, it's like that except it's a forty-five. Same color and everything."

"F---."

"Little bit smaller. Once we have this twenty-two, Bam! Bam! Bam! man, you know?"

"Yeah."

"I bet you we can pop off some of the broads over there."

"Yeah, homes. Hey, don't you have blue bandannas over there somewhere?" Beau asked.

"Nope."

"F---. I got it, just one here. You want to wear that today?"

"I got my beanie. I always wear my beanie."

"I got my black bandanna on."

"Can't start no fights over there . . ."

"I know."

". . . because this f---ing truck's gonna be hot soon."

"We need to get a good chop shop."

"I know one. In Portland."

"Okay."

"I'll call him right now. Want me to?"

"Yeah."

"All right."

"Later."

It was clear to the detectives that Beau Flynn and Sam Warthan were about to take possession of weapons that would be used in a series of burglaries and perhaps robberies as well. But where and when?

JANUARY 17, 1995

The wire was quiet until the next morning at 11:12 a.m. when Beau called his buddy Tom Simmons.

"Hello?" Tom answered.

"What's up?" said Beau. "What're you guys doing?"

"Just taking a shower."

"Yeah, that bitch, she's got it with her."

The cops surmised it was the .22 in question. But who was "the bitch"?

"Yeah, we're gonna hit some houses today," Beau continued.

"Yeah."

"And that way, we don't get smoked if we get in there, you know?"

"Uh huh."

"I'd rather smoke than be smoked."

Smoked meant killed; Beau was saying he'd rather do the killing than be killed and the gun "the bitch" was going to give him would allow him to do just that.

"You know that girl Lisa?"

"Yeah?"

"That one I'm getting it from?"

"Yeah."

The detectives barely heard the rest of the conversation. Now they knew the person giving Beau the revolver was named Lisa and it was a good bet it was Lisa Fentress, whom they knew to be part of the gang. Their hunch was confirmed a few minutes later at 11:39 a.m. when Fentress called Beau.

"Hey, I'm ready," Beau said.

"So you'll be here in like fifteen minutes?" Lisa asked.

"Well, more like twenty or thirty."

"Okay."

"Hey, homes, instead, bring 'em all over to the high school."

"All right."

"And then I'll take 'em."

Beau would be driving a stolen Chevy Suburban wagon. The meeting place was South Eugene High School.

"All right, okay," Lisa said, and the conversation ended.

So that was the scam: Lisa Fentress was delivering the guns to Beau Flynn. The exchange would take place at South Eugene High School, which Lisa attended.

The wiretap was only four days old and already Michaud had evidence of a felony in the making. The decision now was whether to compromise the tap at this early stage and bust Flynn after receiving the guns but before he could take off with them, or follow him after he took possession and see what happened.

It was really no decision at all. Flynn would be arrested as soon as the guns changed hands. No reason to put innocent civilians at risk. And if Mary Thompson then figured out that her son was arrested because of the tap, so be it.

Michaud contacted the patrol officer whose beat was South Eugene High School. He told him to be on the lookout for a stolen Chevy Suburban that was coming to the front of the school, that Beau Flynn would probably be passing guns to a student name of Lisa Fentress. Michaud "suggested" that some patrol officers offer support in case of trouble and to assist in effecting an arrest.

Thirty minutes later, Michaud was still at the listening post while uniformed patrol officers staked out the grounds of South Eugene High School where the exchange would soon take place.

At 12:10, a Chevy Suburban wagon pulled into an open space in front of the school. Quickly, police ran the wagon's plates. They came back stolen. A few minutes later, Lisa Fentress appeared. She walked slowly to the car, glancing nervously around, then got in on the passenger side.

"Close in," the cop in charge radioed.

Beau Flynn, the bright, sad boy, who had grown into a thin, handsome, still-baby-faced young man. Had it been the 1930's, the time of the legendary gangsters whom Beau aspired to emulate, he could easily be known as "Baby Face" Flynn. And like his antecedents, Baby Face Nelson, Pretty Boy Floyd and John Dillinger, Beau Flynn got his kicks from robbing and stealing. The adrenaline rush, the real addiction to the criminal life, that came from the ever-present threat of the police chase.

"Beau Flynn, get out of the car and lie face down on the ground," a police loudspeaker crackled.

Lisa quickly exited the car. After she did, Beau backed up, put the car into gear and floored the accelerator. It is doubtful that even *Car and Driver* had put the Suburban to the test that Beau did now.

Concerned that she might still have the weapons on her, and that she might bring them into the school with her, Lisa was immediately arrested. Upon searching her, police realized that the exchange had already taken place. Not only was Beau fleeing, he was armed and now considered dangerous.

In the listening post, the DNR clicked on as Mary received an incoming call. The caller was a gang wannabe named *Mark Darling*.

"Hello?" Mary answered.

"Who is this?" Mark Darling asked.

"Hello?" Mary repeated.

"Mary?"

"Yeah?"

"Is Beau there?"

"No."

"Hey, what color is the Suburban they got?"

"Blue."

"They're chasing it down Eighteenth."

"Huh?"

"I said they're chasing it down Eighteenth."

"He's in it!"

"Who is?"

"Beau."

"The cops are chasing it down Eighteenth. It's on the scanner right now. He was sitting there when he saw it pass. He just now ran the plate number and it came up stolen."

"It should come up a different plate. Damn!"

Beau had replaced the car's plates with others, so it wouldn't show up stolen.

"He's in it," Darling repeated.

"He is, huh?"

"Yeah."

"Which way they coming down?" Mary asked, her voice rising in alarm.

"They didn't say."

"Have they caught it yet?"

"No, he was just calling in."

"Can they outrun him?"

"I'll call you back in a few minutes. I'm gonna see what they say."

"Okay, honey, thank you."

"Bye."

If it wasn't for the fact that accidents could happen in a high-speed chase, and that Beau had a loaded revolver, if it wasn't for those things, Michaud would have been on the floor rolling in laughter. How bizarre! The cops chasing Beau, and Mary following the whole thing on Darling's scanner.

Outside on the streets of Eugene, Beau was racing from one side of the city to the other. With the cops in pursuit, the Suburban soon got up to 100 miles an hour.

The DNR clicked on. Michaud picked up the phones. It was Darling again.

"Hello?"

"Mary?"

"Yeah."

"It's it," Darling confirmed.

This guy has a way with brevity, Michaud thought.

"They catch 'em?" Mary sounded worried.

"It's an emerald-green car, right?"

"Did they catch him?" Mary asked again, ignoring Mark's question.

"They're right behind it," Darling announced.

"Oh, my God! What'll I do?"

You? Michaud thought. *What about your son?*

"They're on Twentieth and Tyler," Darling continued. "They lost it. He went down an alley. He's running from 'em."

"Oh, God."

"No, they're, they're hauling ass," said Darling, listening intently to his police scanner.

"Oh, God."

Michaud had to admit that this was the first time he'd seen—or, anyway, *heard*—Mary lose her composure.

"Wow!" Darling repeated. "It's a high-speed chase. They're headed back toward your house."

Now Michaud had to laugh. He just had to. Mary must be leaking anxiety at the thought that her son was leading the cops to her!

"I don't know what I can do to help him. I can't help him. That f---in' car is sitting out here," she continued referring to a car stolen by the gang and parked outside her house.

"Yeah, 'cause they changed the plates."

"Damn!"

"The only reason they knew where it was, Mark?"

"Yeah?"

"Is 'cause it was a cop's Suburban. Oh, mutherf---er! The cop left his keys in it."

"Yeah?"

"Get out of it, Beau," Mary screamed, as though Beau could hear her. "Get out of it, Beau!"

"Talk to you later."

"Mark, let me know what's happening."

"I will, Mary. Okay. Bye."

"Bye."

*   *   *

Outside on the street, residents knew something was wrong because you could hear the sirens wailing from one end of Eugene to the other. The last thing cops want in such a circumstance is for civilians to get in the way and, so far, nothing like that had happened. But the longer the chase kept up, the longer there continued the chance that someone would get seriously hurt.

Inside the Suburban, Beau's heart beat wildly in his chest. He was on the adventure of a lifetime and enjoying it immensely.

Across town, inside her house, Mary couldn't stand the suspense. She reached for the phone.

"Hello?" Michaud heard her say. "Is Mark there?"

"This is him."

"Mark, it's Mary, did they catch him?"

There was a pause, probably Darling listening to his scanner.

"No, they're on Eighteenth and Polk now."

"They got . . . it's got that thing?"

"What thing?"

"That stolen thing."

"Oh, the . . ."

"Bang bang."

"Oh, really?" Darling responded, realizing that "bang bang" meant there was a handgun in the car with Beau.

"Yeah."

"Hey, they're on Twelfth and Polk now."

"Oh, my God . . ."

"They've got . . . they're putting a car in front of him to block him off."

"He's in there!"

"I only have one channel, so I probably won't hear the whole conversation."

"F---! Get out of it, Beau, get out of it, Beau," Mary pleaded, as if her wayward son could hear her.

"The only way he's gonna get away is to plow them f---ers."

"How is Beau gonna get out of it?"

"He might as well just plow it! He'll just run the f---ing cops over with it. Ha ha ha ha."

"They gonna send him away." Mary began to cry.

"Yeah, Craig got sent to MacLaren this morning."

"When they sending him up?"

"In a little while."

"Oh, f---," Mary keened, like any concerned mother with the vocabulary of a street thug, "there's not a f---ing thing I can do to help him."

Nope, Michaud thought and smiled again.

"Wait, I think the cops lost them."

"Oh, good," Mary said, sounding joyous, hopeful.

"They better jump out and run, 'cause there're cops waiting on every corner for the f---er."

Michaud could hear the scanner in the background.

"One Adam twelve to units, suspect car is a dark green or teal color."

"Yep, teal," Darling confirmed to no one in particular.

"I hope they know to pull in somebody's driveway and get the f--- out of it," Mary suggested. "And run."

Run, that's a good thing to do, and Michaud sipped his coffee.

"Two charles ten, has the vehicle parked on Almaden north of Twenty-eighth?"

"*The lights are on. I'm gonna stand by here. I can't see if anybody's in it.*"

"He jumped out and ran," Mark advised Mary. "The car, he parked it and took off. He just . . ."

"You got a car?" Mary interrupted.

"Huh?"

"You have a car?"

"No."

"I gotta get to him. I gotta get to him . . ."

"The headlights and everything are on, Mary. They're trying to see if somebody's in it."

"They'll have a problem. It's got tinted windows."

"Well, hold on a minute."

The scanner again.

"*On station, uh, correction, station one two x-ray twenty-three, assign four quadrant cars to that immediate area.*"

"They're sending four cars to look for him," Darling translated.

"Hang on, Beau, hang on. Mark?"

"Yes, Mary?"

"Hang on a minute."

"Yeah, you hold on, I'm gonna listen." The line went dead. Not two seconds later the phone rang again.

"*Mom?*"

Michaud sat bolt upright. It was Beau Flynn.

"Mom, she set us up!"

"Hey! Hey! Where are you?"

"I'm, I'm safe."

"See if you can trace this," Michaud shouted to Rainey, who began to frantically call the phone company to see if they could put a trace on the incoming call.

"The cops are after your ass, son."

"Me?"

"Yeah. I'm hearing it on the scanner. I got Mark listening for me."

"Beau Flynn, huh?" Beau asked. He was hoping that maybe the cops didn't know it was him. No one ever said criminals were the brightest people in the world.

"The cops are after whoever was in the Suburban."

"They don't know who was in it?"

"No."

"All right. What do you want me to do?"

"Where are you?"

Michaud leaned forward, pen at the ready, even though the conversation was being taped.

"Well, I'll get home!"

Damn, Michaud thought. *He's not telling us where he is.*

"Don't—"

"Don't worry," Beau continued to reassure his mother. "F---, we got rid of the Suburban."

"They're getting dogs out after you."

Michaud looked at Rainey. "We are?" Michaud asked.

"I'm coming home," Beau screamed.

"Come home!" Mary wailed, like her son was a Boy Scout lost in the wilderness.

Seconds later, Mary called Mark Darling.

"Mark, he's on his way home."

"They're after him," said Mark, listening. "He's running down the street. Running on Almaden."

"He said Lisa set him up."

"Okay, now they have an ID on him. They're gonna stop 'im."

"Beau said he'll get home," Mary answered hopefully.

"*Subject is seventeen years old, about six-one, not wearing a hat.*"

"He had a hat on," Mary corrected.

"He probably took it off," Mark answered.

"*Two Sam ten, two x-ray twenty-three,*" continued the scanner voice, "*We have information that the suspect is Beau Flynn . . .*"

"Yep, they said his name," said Mark.

"*We have a picture . . .*"

"They have a picture of Beau in their car, Mary."

"*Flynn dropped off a girl in front of South Eugene High School.*"

"That'd be Lisa," Mark answered.

"Yep," said Mary. "But she said it was Beau Flynn, huh?"

Now *that* was good news to Michaud. That meant Mary still didn't suspect the wiretap.

"No, they, the cops have a picture of him. Some lady cop. And she goes, 'Yeah, I believe it's Beau Flynn. I have a picture of him right here.'"

"Okay, let me call you right back."

"Okay, bye."

And Mary was true to her word. She called Mark back in minutes.

"They know it was Beau Flynn," said Mark.

"They know for sure?" Mary asked, sounding very worried now that her son had been positively identified. "How do they know for sure?"

"I don't know. Wait, I'm listening. Ugh, they say there's twenty-two ammunition all over the vehicle, that he's armed. They got twenty-two long-rifle shells in the Suburban."

"I don't know what to do," said Mary, sounding real worried. Her worry made Michaud feel *real* good. The tide was turning.

"Did you call your husband, John?"

"I paged him and I tried his cell phone and he hasn't called me back. Oh, my God!" And she hung up, only to call Darling out of nervousness a few minutes later.

"Witnesses saw him jump out of the vehicle," Darling reported.

"Who's the witness?" Mary asked.

Michaud and Rainey looked at each other.

"Whoever's house they parked in front of."

"Oh. Do they have him?"

"No, not yet. They can't find him."

At that moment, *Doris Schneider* happened to be looking out the back door of her home and saw a young man fleeing across her lawn. She immediately called police.

"Some lady just called and said there's somebody in her backyard," Mark reported.

"Oh, God!"

Mary didn't know what to do, so she hung up. A moment later Larry Martin called.

"Where are you?" asked Mary.

"I'm at home," Larry responded.

"Lisa turned 'im in."

Michaud smiled broadly and took the headphones away from his ear. "I think our worrying about compromising the wire was for nothing," said Michaud. Rainey, who had continued to listen, motioned to the headphones and Michaud put them back on.

"Yeah. The cops are chasing him through the south hills as we speak," said Mary.

"Damn! Did she turn me in too?" Martin asked.

"Huh?"

"Did she say diddley about me too?"

"I don't know."

" 'Cause I'm gonna f---ing disappear right now."

"I don't know what she said."

"Stay calm. Take a pill. Take two pills. Damn . . ."

He hung up and a few minutes later, Mary phoned Mark Darling.

"What's happening?"

"They're trying to find the lady that called in so she can identify 'im."

"Is he in custody?"

"I'm not sure. It's confusing."

"I'm thinking maybe we should drive up around there."

"If you go up there and look for him, leave your cellular on so if they say something I can call ya."

"Okay, bye."

It had not been a good day for Beau Flynn. First, someone informed on him. Then a wild chase with the cops in pursuit from South Eugene into East Eugene. Then getting out when the cops were closing in, and now, the dragnet was out for him. But he was nothing if not resourceful.

Beau managed to make it to Sam Warthan's house. He talked Sam into driving him out of the police search area. Cops, though, had set up roadblocks and when Sam pulled his car abreast of the police stop, no amount of hiding on Beau's part could stop the cops from identifying him.

Taken into custody, police found the .22 caliber pistols Lisa had handed him under the back seat. Mary got there in time to see her son already captured, hands cuffed behind his back, in police custody.

"Ma!" Beau screamed, as he was being shoved into the back seat of a squad car.

"Beau!" Mary screamed back.

Local stations regularly monitor the police frequency. One of them had heard the chase and capture on the police scanner and had already arrived with a camera crew. The reporter had seen the exchange between Mary and Beau.

"Turn it on," the petite, titian-haired reporter said to her cameraman. "Let's go." Carrying the equipment, trailed by the cameraman, she went up to Mary and shoved the mike in her face. On came the light on top of the camera and for a moment, Mary was blinking, blinded by the light.

"You're 'Gang Mom,' aren't you?"

"Well—"

"Our station did a story about you."

"I—"

"Is Beau Flynn your son?"

Mary muttered something, and then said: "If you don't get that muthaf---ing camera out of my face, I'm gonna break your muthaf---ing camera!"

She pushed the reporter out of the way and barreled up to the squad car. The window was open. Beau leaned forward, his head barely making it to the open window.

"Keep your mouth shut!" Mary whispered, and then

the car, with siren wailing, drove away through the crowd.

"What are you arresting him for?" Mary asked a plainclothes cop.

"I can't talk to you," the cop answered.

"Hey, wait a minute . . ."

Mary tried using her status as "Gang Mom" to get the cops to talk to her, but to no avail. All they would say was that Beau was being taken downtown for questioning.

With nothing to do until Beau was processed through the system, Mary returned home. At 4:08 p.m. the DNR came on; Michaud and Rainey reached for their headphones.

"Hey, is Mary there?"

"Hold on," said a voice, probably her husband John, who had answered.

"Hello?" said Mary.

"Hi," said Lisa Fentress. And then she giggled. "Did you hear what happened?" She giggled some more. "Did you hear what happened?"

"Yeah, and I don't think it's very f---ing funny either," Mary answered dryly.

"Neither do I," said Lisa, sobering up. "Like, what happened?"

"All I know is Beau is sitting in custody."

"Why? What for?"

"I don't know," Mary answered suspiciously. "They won't tell me."

"That's f---ing up, 'cause he . . ."

"What did they ask you?"

Mary still thought it was Lisa who had turned Beau

in but she wanted to pump her to see what she had given the police.

"They asked me who was in the car and I was like, 'I don't know. I was just giving directions.' And they asked, 'Well, was Beau Flynn in the car?' And I said, 'I never said that.' And they're like, 'Why do you hang out with people like that?' I'm like, 'Beau's turning his f---ing life around and he's going to college and stuff.' And they're like, 'Well, then, why was he in the car?' And I go, 'I never said he was in the car. I want my lawyer!' And they took me, handcuffed me and stuff, took me to City Hall and they arrested me. And then they took me back to school and they might press charges for stealing a car."

"Were you in the car?"

"Kind of."

"Just giving them directions?"

"Yeah."

"Just don't say anything."

"I know, I was giving directions. I didn't really look at him. I was just giving directions. On how to get to Spencer Butte Middle School."

"Okay."

"I'm gonna sue 'em. They f---ing . . ."

Mary barely heard the rest of what Lisa said, so keen was her anxiety about what was happening to Beau. It was anxiety well-placed.

Remanded to the custody of juvenile court, Beau was quickly charged with conspiracy to commit burglary. Pending disposition of the charges, he was sent back to MacLaren for violating his parole. He would eventually be tried and convicted as an adult and sentenced to five years in the state penitentiary. He would finally have to do hard time for his crimes.

To Michaud, murder was the ultimate game. And he was losing it. Mary Thompson's hold over those kids was allowing her to get away with murder. It wasn't so much that he liked Aaron Iturra, though his mother seemed to be a good person. And while it would be nice to effect an arrest because it might help Janyce sleep better at night, that wasn't the real reason he wanted to get Mary.

Michaud just hated, *hated*, any criminal who thought she was smarter than he was. And he had one more shot to show Mary who was smarter. If he didn't win, she would get away with murder.

I better not blow it, he thought. *I better be right that we find out what she's really like when we listen in.*

At first Mary Thompson did suspect that it was Lisa Fentress who was the snitch, but over the next month, as her paranoia waxed and waned, her suspicions fell on other members of the gang. Such was her feeling that she was above the law that she never once suspected the truth. The proof of that was that she kept talking and Michaud kept listening.

By February, after the wire had been in place a month, Michaud figured he'd heard enough to get an indictment for aggravated murder, that is, Mary Thompson had caused Aaron Iturra's death through her actions. It wasn't murder one, but it was as close as he could get, and with a conviction, she would go to jail for life. After consulting with Skelton, the decision was made to conclude the tap, arrest Mary and present their evidence at trial. But first the evidence would be secretly presented before a grand jury to secure an indictment.

That turned out to be just a formality; the grand jury came back with the indictment immediately.

The night before her arrest, Michaud once more stood on the porch of his house. It was winter now and it had been raining for weeks. Usually, he found something soothing about the rain. It was never too cold in the Willamette River Valley and when it rained, it was a tranquil time.

As he sipped his martini, Michaud felt anything but tranquil. He wondered if he'd done all that he could to secure a conviction. Nothing was ever certain with a jury. He was watching the Simpson case down in Los Angeles with interest because he had worked before with Marcia Clark and Mark Fuhrman and wasn't overly impressed with either. And there was a case where they had Simpson open and shut, touchdown, and he could certainly see a way they could screw things up. He just hoped that he was not being overconfident, that he had done his job.

The wiretaps after the car chase—another parallel to Simpson, but the Eugene version was high-speed—had shown that Mary Thompson had engaged in a criminal conspiracy to prey on the people of Eugene. Drug deals, burglaries, gun deals, it was all part of the same pattern of criminal behavior that had led Michaud to form his theory that Beau and Mary were more than mother and son: they were business partners.

Their gang had preyed on Eugene's citizens, which he felt accounted for the increase in selected categories of crime. It was Michaud's hope that with her off the street, the numbers would start going down. But the prize here wasn't in bringing down a racketeering gangster so much as it was bringing down a cold-blooded murderer.

Not too far away, Mary Thompson was settling into bed with her husband John. She figured she had done all that she could to obscure her participation in the murder of Aaron Iturra and the criminal activities of the 74 Hoover Crips. She believed that since nothing had happened to her so far, nothing would. Well, maybe some sort of charge of obstructing justice, but nothing more serious than that.

No, she was beginning to feel optimistic about the future.

WOMAN CHARGED IN ITURRA MURDER
Mary Thompson, an outspoken critic of youth gangs, is charged with aggravated murder.

On Friday, February 11, 1995, the headline of *The Register Guard*, Eugene's leading paper, said it all. Mary had been arrested and charged in a grand jury indictment with aggravated murder, first degree burglary, first degree theft and six counts of hindering prosecution. She was remanded to Lane County Jail without bail, pending arraignment.

To the embarrassment of certain members of the Eugene Police Department, the article pointed out the following:

"Thompson . . . was generally looked upon by police, reporters and community leaders as a knowledgeable and outspoken opponent of gang activity. She frequently used the story of her own son's path into gang life as a tool to discourage youngsters from criminal behavior while persuading parents that gangs aren't just a big city problem. Her family's story was told in a front-page story in *The Register Guard* in December 1993."

Michaud put down the paper. It was still a long haul. With pre-trial motions and such, it could take a year or more before they went to trial. He picked up the paper again and gazed at Mary's mug shot, which graced the article, and allowed himself the luxury of feeling just a little bit good.

In her cell at Lane County Jail, Mary Thompson was a celebrity. Mary basked in the good feelings toward her. She was "Gang Mom," and the other prisoners gave her the respect they felt she was due. All except one.

She hated *Kristen Clooney* and Kristen hated her. Bunk mates, they were both big, bluff, domineering women. Kristen thought Mary got special treatment from the guards because of her celebrity status. And she hated the way Mary bragged, especially the way she made threats.

"If I'm convicted," Mary boasted, "I'll make Aaron's mother dead too."

As for the possibility of conviction, Mary remained optimistic, and why not? As 1995 dragged on, she saw O.J. Simpson acquitted with far more evidence than she figured the district attorney had on her. It was only a matter of time and she'd be on the street once again.

TWELVE

BY THE SUMMER OF 1996, Maya Iturra, Aaron's sister, had attempted suicide by slashing her wrists. Maya felt that she was responsible for Aaron's death.

After all, she had taken the call from Lisa Fentress and told her that Aaron was home. Had she not done that, her brother would still be alive, she reasoned.

A psychotherapist put Maya on anti-depression medication and her condition improved. She continued to go to therapy, as did her siblings, who had been left with tremendous reserves of unresolved feelings over Aaron's death. This all put that much more pressure on Janyce to hold things together, which she did, while going to therapy herself.

Alternately, Janyce would feel that she had overcome the grief over her son's death, only to plunge back into the dark abyss of depression. Up and down it went. But mid-June would see the trial of Mary Thompson and Janyce's thoughts began to focus on one thing and one thing alone:

Revenge.

It had been Mary Thompson who brought this blight on her family and now, now, she wanted to see Mary Thompson get hers.

Across town, Jim Michaud was thinking along the

same lines, though without that depth of feeling. While he, also, wanted Mary Thompson punished, he was too seasoned a product of the system to expect that would happen. Even if she were incarcerated for life, would that bring Aaron back? If he had it his way, she would go to the death chamber and have her veins filled with poison and die a slow, agonizing death. Again, reality intruded.

First, death by injection was looked at by the penal system as one of the more humane methods to put a murderer out. No pain. Just fall asleep and never wake up.

Second, and more important, because Mary was charged with *contributing* to Aaron's death, that is, not actually having pulled the trigger herself, the best the state could hope for was a conviction on aggravated murder, which in Oregon was only punishable by life imprisonment. Other states had more restrictive laws where Mary could have been charged with murder one and faced death. Not Oregon.

Finally, Michaud was too pragmatic to expect that, no matter how good the state's case was, a jury would automatically convict. The Simpson verdict was less than a year old and in everyone's mind; it had proven that, however strong your case was, you could find a selected group of twelve morons who would choose to ignore what was right in front of them and opt for an innocent verdict.

With all these things in mind, Michaud, ever the idealist tilting at windmills, decided, with the approval of his superiors, to attend the trial and offer Skelton whatever support he might during the proceedings. It was a duty he was only too eager to perform because, above all else, Mary Thompson had violated the law, and to a lawman like Michaud, she had to be convicted, plain and simple.

As for Steve Skelton, he was the one who would be prosecuting the case on behalf of the state. Skelton always felt pressure when trying a big case, and on the "Gang Mom" case in particular, with all of its attendant publicity, he felt the pressure most acutely.

Mary Thompson was a significant threat to the community. She was a murderer who had yet to be convicted and if she wasn't, he was afraid she would keep on killing to reach her criminal goals of maintaining her gang's power. For that reason and that reason alone, he wanted to win.

Of course, there was pressure on the state to do a thoroughly professional job. The community was watching and if the media had its way, they'd be watching very closely. And with that kind of microscopic scrutiny, the state needed to win. To do that, they had to present a case without mistakes to the jury.

Skelton had an interesting way of trying cases. He tried them by memory. He may not have been "The Amazing Kreskin," but he had a memory that allowed him to remember what people said, so he tended to keep a lot of facts in his head. In a case like "Gang Mom," with thousands of pages of intercepts and police reports, he was close to having memorized all of it by the time the case came to trial.

He hoped that his memory would be good enough to construct a case that the jury would believe, and that Mary Thompson would be convicted.

JUNE 13, 1996

The trial of Mary Thompson on the charge of aggravated murder in the death of Aaron Benjamin Iturra began on a bright summer's day. After a jury selection process that lasted three days, a jury of six men, six women and two alternates were seated to hear the case.

Sitting at the prosecution table to the left of Lane County Circuit Judge Lyle Velure was Steve Skelton. On the right, at the defense table, sat a prim, proper and bespectacled Mary Thompson. Next to her was Steve Chez, a noted Portland defense attorney she had retained to defend her against the state's charges. Michaud sat in the back, listening to every word.

"The purpose of the opening statement," Skelton explained to the jury, "is to outline the important facts of the case," which he proceeded to do in short order. He outlined Mary's involvement in the murder, from her requesting and sanctioning it, to helping Brown dispose of the murder weapon.

The 74 Hoover Crips, he explained, "were a very dangerous group of people," perpetrating crimes on the citizens of Eugene, "and the leader of that group was Mary Louise Thompson. Now, the other purpose of the opening statement is to educate you on the law," Skelton continued, explaining that once the state proved their case, the jury would have no alternative but to convict Mary Thompson of aggravated murder.

When it was his turn, Chez presented another view of the case. He argued forcefully that Thompson's actions and motives were entirely misunderstood.

"Mary Thompson treated the gang members with kindness and respect. She was a positive source for these kids. If you didn't know how to talk to them or know their language, there was no talking. She tried to be a positive force, but she had to have realistic goals," Chez continued, explaining that the young people were "nobodies" in society's eyes and that they overcompensated for their inferiority complexes by being "bad" and bragging about crimes that never took place. "There was no jumping-in ceremony," he maintained.

In fact, because these kids had such rich fantasy lives, Mary Thompson initially didn't believe Elstad and Brown's claims of killing Aaron Iturra.

"The twenty-two caliber pistol that Lisa Fentress had was not given to her by Mary Thompson." As for the way she was treated, "Over time, Mary's opinion about law enforcement changed, especially when she came in contact with Jim Michaud."

But I didn't kill anybody, Michaud thought in the back of the courtroom.

Chez continued: "Police were using their vast power with the gang members to get Thompson. 'Tell us something that we can use against Mary Thompson,' they pressured all of the kids they interviewed. Angel Elstad, who you'll hear as a state's witness, was involved in crime," Chez pointed out, and she agreed to testify only because, "Police have the ability to make her life rough. And remember that the state has the power to grant immunity and other deals" with reputed gang members in order to coerce them to testify.

"Mary Thompson did not in any way request or sanction Iturra's death," Chez continued. When she found out what had happened, she felt tremendous guilt because she felt she could have stopped it from happening. It was that guilt she would have to live with for the rest of her life, not the guilt of causing the young man's death.

JUNE 14

All through the year leading up to the trial, Michaud, Rainey and the other detectives who worked the case had interviewed the gang members, working quietly behind the scenes to get them to implicate Mary. Chez's arguments to the contrary, most had been promised nothing in return for their cooperation. Promises really weren't necessary anyway because most had neither committed nor been charged with any crime. What the detectives had, in effect, done was to de-brainwash them, and make them realize that Mary was anything but their friend. Instead, she was a scheming adult bent on benefiting from their criminal activities! And if they happened to be caught, they would just have to take one for the team while she continued to enjoy the spoils of their criminal acts.

The first gang member to take the stand was Linda Miller. She related a conversation she had had with Mary on January 14, 1995. Michaud recalled that the DNR had turned on a little after midnight.

> "So anyway, it got all messed up and they know I know more than what I'm saying," Mary began.
> "Same with me, but there's no way they can prove it," said Linda.
> "But they're trying to f---ing indict me because of what Jim said. About me telling Jim to go do it."
> Mary, her paranoia kicking in, was convinced Jim

had ratted her out to the cops, but nothing could be further from the truth.

"And my alibi is tight for that Sunday," Mary continued. " 'Cause Angel told them that I went over there for an hour and talked to Jim."

"Uh huh."

"And told him it needed to be done. Soon."

"Uh huh."

"And I never went over there, Linda."

"Why would you go over to their house and say something like that?" Linda agreed. "I mean that's gotta be a little obvious. 'Cause they got police reports. They got the police reports all screwed up too."

"Mary often brought up the subject herself about getting Aaron killed," Linda testified in court. "She wanted Aaron capped so he couldn't testify against Beau about his role in the knife fight."

At the defense table, Mary sneered at Linda but she seemed to squirm just a little.

"Mary originally recruited my boyfriend Wayde Hudson to do the job. She told Wayde he had to take care of his 'family.' Mary phoned me ten minutes before the shooting and again afterward."

It was particularly damning testimony but Chez thought she was a liar and was determined to counter it.

During his cross-examination, Linda copped an attitude. Arms folded protectively across her chest, she gave monosyllabic answers. When she bothered to put more than one syllable together, her answers to Chez's questions formed the labored phraseology of "I don't know."

Chez's strategy had been to try to show the discrepancies in her story and her memories but it was proving difficult going because of her intransigence. When he asked her why she implicated Thompson in court after telling her during the January 14 phone conversation, "I know you didn't tell them to do it," Linda was vague in her response. Asked why she lied about her testimony to the grand jury investigating Thompson's role in Aaron's murder, Linda gave various explanations for the discrepancies: she lied to win Mary's trust; she lied because she feared for her safety and her family's safety; "She was the one who went to the police and told on everybody. Why should I tell the truth to someone who didn't tell me the truth?" Linda asked Chez.

Linda recalled that she hung out at Mary's house where, three days prior to the murder, she saw Angel Elstad there with a .38 tucked in the waistband of her pants. Linda said she took the gun from Angel for Angel's safety, then gave it to Thompson at the request of gang member Larry Martin.

"Me, Mary and 'Truth' [Martin] went into the bedroom and Mary handed the gun over to Truth in a holster. Mary said it was the weapon that would take care of our problem."

Linda went on to say that she was afraid of the gang members after the killing, claiming that Truth threatened that ". . . whoever talked was going to be taken care of" in the same way Aaron was.

Chez felt her fears were groundless. Asked if she had had second thoughts about being present when her gang friends were laying out the plot to kill Iturra, she answered with a reluctant "No."

JUNE 18

Wayde Hudson, all of seventeen years old and already a gang veteran, took the stand.

Hudson related how, in September 1994, at the beginning of burning season, Mary Thompson drove to a local park and watched as one teen after another was jumped into the gang she had formed, the 74 Hoover Crips. He said that he, Joe Brown and Lisa Fentress were all jumped in on that night.

"Mary had a certain routine I guess she wanted done, an order of the people she wanted beaten in," Hudson testified under direct examination by prosecutor Steve Skelton. Mary let him join up without being beaten because he said he'd lie to the cops about Beau's involvement in the knife fight. Hudson figured he could take the blame himself because, being a minor, it wasn't such a big thing.

After she accepted him into the gang, Mary gave him the blue rag. "She told me to treat it like my best friend, like it's part of me, and to never let anyone disrespect it."

Mary went on to "freak out" over Beau's arrest and truly believed that Aaron was lying about Beau's involvement in the knife fight. Hudson said that while gang members hung out at Mary's house, where they drank and took drugs, Mary told them that they should ". . . take care of business. At first it was like, we thought she meant beating Aaron up but after some of the gang got a stolen thirty-eight," what she really wanted was Aaron killed.

"At first, Mary chose me and another guy to do it. She would come to me and say, 'We have to take care of business, court's coming up. He can't testify.' " Soon after that, Hudson maintained, he started to leave the gang's sphere of influence. "I didn't want to be around it [the gang] because it was getting out of control. I knew something was going to happen," a fact he was assured of when, a few days before the murder, he heard his best friend, Jim Elstad, and Crazy Joe Brown say that they ". . . were going to be the ones taking care of business."

The tape of Mary's statement to Rainey and Raynor was played for the jury, followed by Mary's conversation the same day with Angel Elstad in which Angel told Mary, "You said it needed to get done and it needed to get done soon."

With the afternoon moving on toward evening, the judge recessed court till morning.

JUNE 19

Hudson once again took the witness stand, and Skelton continued his direct examination.

Hudson testified that he'd lied to detectives when he was originally interviewed. At that time, he had told them that Mary had tried to persuade the gang members to forget about murdering Aaron. He also stated that he lied when he said that Mary had had no role in the murder. At the time of his interview, he was in juvenile jail and didn't want to be labeled a "snitch."

Under Chez's skillful cross-examination Hudson admitted, "She never said 'Kill him.' It was kind of like beating around the bush. It was pretty obvious what she meant." Still, aggravated murder required intent and if the state could not prove that, Chez knew the jury would have no choice but to acquit.

Hudson went on to say that he didn't learn that Thompson had implicated Brown and Elstad until January 1995, because at that time, he was in the Skipworth Juvenile Detention Center, where news of the outside world was sometimes received a little late. Chez, challenging Hudson's reasons for testifying against Mary, asked him if the news had made him angry.

"Yes," he said. "In my opinion, a lot of what happened was her fault . . . and she goes around and gets everybody else in trouble." He wanted revenge against Mary. And, if the jury bought that, they would have to disregard his testimony.

After Hudson finished, Skelton scanned his witness list and decided to throw in a curve ball. There were more gang members who'd testify, but he thought it might be interesting to hear first from someone else who knew Mary.

"The state calls Kristine Clooney to the stand."

He was determined to show the jury that Mary Thompson's predilection toward murder was not just one isolated instance and to do that, he needed Clooney's testimony.

"Raise your right hand and repeat after me. Do you swear to tell the truth, the whole truth and nothing but the truth, so help you God?" intoned the court clerk.

"I do," Clooney answered, and took her seat in the witness box.

As large and tough-looking a woman as Mary, Clooney had been "Gang Mom"'s bunk mate in Lane County Jail from December 1995 to May 1996. While Mary occupied bunk number 14, Clooney was only a few beds away.

"She [Mary] said if she were convicted, she'd make sure Aaron's mother [Janyce] was dead too," Clooney stated. "She wrote a rap song about the murder itself and how she was like O.J. and would be acquitted."

Clooney claimed that some of the jail's deputies coddled Mary, perhaps because of her status as a celebrity defendant or her past work as an anti-gang activist. Because of this, Mary's subsequent behavior was tolerated.

"One minute she'd be crying, the next she'd be throwing things around. Her mood swings were to the extreme. She also got herself assigned the easy laundry duty and always chose blankets, sheets and pillow cases for herself in blue, her gang's *rag* color."

In cross-examining Clooney, Chez got her to admit that she was in jail on theft and forgery charges, and that she had a long criminal history, including armed robbery. Then, Chez wondered, did the state offer her any sort of deal in return for her testimony?

"No, I haven't been offered leniency for anything," Clooney answered. "Look, my life isn't a pretty picture. But I take responsibility for what I've done. I'm real tired and I'm trying to turn my life around."

Still, Clooney wasn't the best of witnesses. She admitted under cross-examination that she never trusted Mary, that they never got along, and that she neither liked nor trusted other women. "I have a high animosity toward any woman," she said. It would be left to a therapist on a distant day in the future to figure out exactly what that was all about.

Mary had boasted about her gang to Clooney and another woman, jail deputy Jean Petersen, who testified the same day. "Mary carried on about how Crips were better people" than police officers and how "her son is a Crip and he's the best Crip there is," Petersen testified. "She said, 'All I have to do is make one little phone call and this community could be hurt real bad.'"

JUNE 20

"They'll never be able to hang me because my homies won't talk," Sam Warthan testified that Mary Thompson had said during a conversation with him and Beau in January 1995. He said that he, Thompson and Flynn were in a car when he and Flynn began horsing around. When he jokingly bragged about beating up Flynn, Thompson told him not to mess "with us because look what happened to Aaron." Then he recounted a later conversation during which, "Me, Beau and Mark were *jockey-boxing* [breaking into cars and stealing stereos] a few days before Beau got caught when we spotted a Chevy Suburban with the keys inside."

They stole the car and then drove around Eugene until they found a matching vehicle so they could switch license plates and thus fool the police into believing the car wasn't stolen.

Skelton then played the tapes of Beau's conversations on January 17 with Lisa Fentress regarding picking up the .22 at South Eugene High School, and then the tapes of Mary's conversations with Mark Darling recounting the subsequent car chase and capture. The jury did not seem visibly moved by Mary's crying as recorded on the tapes.

JUNE 21

Skelton's strategy seemed to be paying off. The jury had listened attentively as the gang members testified. Now it was time to have Mary Thompson convict herself with her own words. With the court's permission, Skelton was allowed to play some of the wiretaps recorded subsequent to Beau's capture.

On some of the tapes in which Mary spoke to gang members, she expressed ignorance about Beau's activities when he was caught. "All he [Beau] was doing was getting a ride to school," she told Lisa Fentress during one conversation, a lie repeated in a number of subsequent conversations. Other wiretaps showed that she was deliberately lying to gang members in order to manipulate them, that she knew the Suburban was stolen, that the plates had been changed and that Beau was heading to meet Lisa for the gun exchange.

At one point while Beau was speaking with Lisa, you could hear Mary get on the line, urging Lisa to give him the gun. During another conversation, Mary admitted alibiing Beau, telling cops that Beau was asleep in her house at the time of the chase.

Mary worried about Beau being sent back to MacLaren, and about her own future too, because of the pressure police were putting on gang members to testify against her. On the tapes, she sounded paranoid and scared, though sometimes she did a 180-degree turn and just seemed to laugh everything off, as if nothing had happened and nothing mattered.

"If I were going to get hooked up for murder, they'd have come and got me already," she said in one call. In another, she was recorded as follows:

MACHINE: Hi. You have reached 555-9039. Sorry we're unable to take your call, but please don't hang up. Leave your name, number and a short message and we'll get back to you.

THOMPSON: Yo. It's the murderous brainwashing bitch here and it's Saturday and if you get a chance, give me a call. Bye.

JUNE 25

The first witness of the morning was one of Mary's foremost allies: Angel Elstad, the older sister of the "shooter," Jim Elstad.

By the time Angel took the stand, she was twenty years old, and trying to turn her life around by attending Lane Community College, where she was a sophomore. Since her first child was born, on the night Aaron died, she had given birth to another who was now five months old.

"How many times had you been to Mary Thompson's house with your brother?" Skelton asked.

"About ten to twenty times with Jim," Angel answered.

"To the best of your knowledge, when were the Seventy-four Hoover Crips formed?"

"About one to one-and-a-half months before Aaron died."

"And were you 'jumped in' at that time?"

"No, I was eight months pregnant then."

"What did Mary Thompson mean by 'taking care of' Aaron Iturra?"

"That meant that Aaron couldn't testify against Beau."

"And how did she incite the gang against Aaron?"

"Well, first, she claimed that Aaron snuck over the fence to her house and poisoned her dog Lars. Second, she said Aaron was involved in selling drugs to little kids and third that he was having sex with little kids. But see, she would be, like, talking about all that and then I remember a lady arrived at Mary's house in the middle of the day and the conversation changed to gang intervention."

"It was like she was another person?"

"It was a complete contrast," Angel agreed.

"Did Mary Thompson have a gang background?"

"Mary said that she'd been a Crip for thirty years and that she kept a can of spent bullets she used in her life under a floorboard in her house."

"Did she tell you to wear your gang rags?"

"All the time. You were supposed to wear your rags all the time. Mary said, 'Don't let anyone mess with the rags.' "

"What about John Thompson, did he know what was happening?"

"No, he was at work. We had private meetings where kids did drugs like crack. The kids would come back from the back bedroom where Mary was, rubbing their noses."

"Was there a burglary Mary masterminded?"

Angel nodded.

"At the Pleasant Hill gun shop. Mary told [the gang members] the specific guns to steal. I was driving the getaway car and everyone got cold feet when a police officer drove by."

"What about Jim? What kind of relationship did he have with Mary?"

"We have a difference of opinion. Mary Thompson was his 'Moms.' See, Jim changed around August [of 1994]. We used to be involved with rock slides and swimming and just hanging out." Then he started hanging with Mary and began declining. Eventually, Mary had such a hold on him that "if Mary asked him to do something, there was nothing on God's green earth that could stop him from doing it." Angel described her brother and the other teens as being pressured into taking care of Aaron for Mary.

Throughout Angel's testimony, Mary scribbled notes to Chez, uttering profanity under her breath. Angel went on to describe how she heard the shot that killed Aaron, how her brother and Joe Brown showed up a few minutes later.

"What happened then?" Skelton wondered.

"A zillion things were coming out of their mouths a million miles a minute," Angel testified. When she asked Jim why he had killed Aaron, "He said from conversations he'd had earlier with Mary that my [unborn] son would have gotten killed if he hadn't taken care of it." After that, they all went over to Mary's.

Under cross-examination, Chez got Angel to admit that she thought Thompson, her brother and Crazy Joe merely intended to beat Aaron up. But noting that Aaron was a big guy they couldn't just lean on, she assumed they'd threaten him. "I figured they'd say something and Aaron would put them in their place and they would come home. I didn't even think he'd get a scratch." She admitted knowing that Brown had stolen a .38 caliber revolver, but didn't think he'd use it.

"And you knew this gun?" Chez asked.

"Yes, I'd borrowed it a few days before and drove to Mapleton to scare this kid that was threatening my cousin."

Angel wasn't such an angel after all, which was exactly what Chez was trying to establish.

"Did you ever hear Mary Thompson say she wanted Aaron Iturra murdered?"

"No," Angel answered.

"Shortly after the murder, you had a phone conversation with Mary Thompson in which you said that you knew your brother and Brown were going to 'cap' Aaron the night he died, right?"

"Well, I can't remember any of that. I was heavily medicated after my delivery. The details about the day of the murder and the days afterward are all just a blur. Maybe I was trying to impress the detective at that time. I couldn't tell you. My attitude was just very childish and just stupid, plain stupid."

"Did you believe that Mary Thompson would kill your brother James if he tried to leave the Seventy-four Hoover Crips?"

"You bet!" she practically shouted. "I overheard Jim say that he would be killed in a conversation before the murder with our mom. She was urging him to stop his gang stuff."

Chez had apparently made the one mistake lawyers are never supposed to: he had asked a question without knowing what the answer would be in advance.

"Did you really believe she had a can of bullets under the floor boards?"

"Yes."

"Did you participate in conversations against Aaron Iturra?"

"Perhaps. I think I stood up for Aaron." Angel concluded, "It was all centered around her. Our family was nothing."

THIRTEEN

NEXT UP TO THE stand was gang member Cameron Slade.

Quickly, Skelton established in his early questioning that Cameron was eighteen years old, living in nearby Klamath County with his girlfriend, that the last grade he attended was the tenth and that he was unemployed.

"What kind of relationship did you have with Mary Thompson?" Skelton continued.

"I considered her to be 'Moms,' " the teenager answered.

He said that Elstad hung around Mary constantly, that he snorted drugs in the back room with the other teens. Skelton was curious as to why Elstad carried out Thompson's bidding.

"Jim would get respect if he killed Aaron Iturra," he answered simply.

"Did you know what was going to happen that night?"

"Yes, I knew it would happen." Afterwards, "When I saw Jim that night, he had his blue bandanna across his face and one over his head. Both Jim and Joe were very excited when they came back to the house." Then they all drove over to Mary's. At first, he watched them go into Mary's house, but when Angel began having labor pains, he went in to get them. Inside the house, he heard Mary on the phone.

"She was telling someone, I don't know who, that 'It was done,' " Cameron said. As they were leaving to take Angel to the hospital, Mary said to Jim and Joe, "Good job," and warned him, Cameron, not to talk. "She said not to say anything about this [the murder]."

Then Steve Chez took over for cross-examination.

"Were you a member of the gang?"

"I was asked to join the gang by Mary but I didn't because I thought gangs were stupid."

"Aren't you concerned over your legal exposure?"

"No, because I didn't encourage anything."

"When did you first find out Mary went to the police?"

"I didn't know she did do that."

"Did you know Beau?"

"No."

"Did you know Joe Brown?"

"I did not like Joe Brown. Jim Elstad was my friend."

On redirect, Cameron admitted that the original idea was to beat Aaron up but once a gun was obtained, killing became the goal.

"Did you ever see Mary Thompson processing drugs?" Skelton asked.

"I saw her melt down the drugs in a spoon," he testified.

It seemed that Mary had not left her drug-processing past behind her when she moved to Eugene from Josephine County.

"One more question. Why was the jumping-in ceremony videotaped?"

"So Mary could mail it to Beau at MacLaren," Slade concluded.

Throughout the trial, in addition to local reporters, the courtroom was packed with scribes from Portland and surrounding localities. The Associated Press had their correspondent there; the Iturra case was going out on the wires around the world. The "Gang Mom" trial was big news.

On the third day of the trial, Skelton stood and intoned, "The state calls Neil Crannell to the stand." A tall, distinguished-looking man in a gray suit came forward and put his hand on the Bible.

"Do you swear to tell the truth, the whole truth and nothing but the truth, so help you God?" asked the court clerk.

"I do," said Crannell, and took his seat in the jury box, while Skelton took his by the lectern. Unlike on television, attorneys are rarely allowed to approach the witness and must do their examining from lecterns across the courtroom.

"Please state your full name."

"Neil Crannell."

"And, Mr. Crannell, how and where are you employed?"

"I am employed in Portland as a policeman for twenty-one years."

"Mr. Crannell, do you have any special expertise?"

"I do. I have testified more than ten times as an expert on gang activities. And I've been a gang intelligence officer for four and a half years. I've interviewed over four hundred gang members in both formal and informal format in both Portland and Los Angeles. I also do training of other police agencies, communities and school settings, et cetera. I was a detective for three years, dealing with violent crimes and primarily black gang activities."

"Your Honor, I'd like the witness admitted as an expert on gang activities."

"Mr. Chez?"

"No objection, Your Honor."

"Now, Mr. Crannell, can you tell us a little bit more about how street gangs are constituted?"

"Most street gangs are divided along racial lines. The Seventy-four Hoover Crips in Portland are all black, there are no whites nor Hispanics. The Crips have their roots in South Central Los Angeles. Another word for gang is *set*. The Seventy-four Hoovers are a *set*. They got their name from where Seventy-fourth and Hoover Streets cross in L.A. The name transferred to Portland, when gang members from California migrated north, bringing their gang mentality and name with them."

"And can you tell us how big gang sets tend to be?"

"Gang sets vary in size. In Portland, the Bloods having fifty to seventy-five members, the Seventy-four Crips between ten and twenty. It's hard to tell how many members there are, some may be in jail, out of town, whatever."

"Could you please define for the court what exactly a street gang is?"

"A street gang is often loosely organized, claiming a specific name and territory. All are involved in criminal activity, use of hand signs and insignia to identify themselves, such as *do-rags*. The *rag* is the flag of the particular gang, and worn with pride. However, the rags are not worn as much anymore, as they are quite visible, and the police and rival gangs see them as a target."

"How does one become a gang member?"

"Well," Crannell continued, shifting a little in his seat, "first, it depends upon racial make-up and geographic area. One tends to join a neighborhood gang where one has grown up. Actual initiation occurs during the *jumping in*, wherein the initiate has to stand through a beating until the *OG* declares he has *heart*. Jumping in is not seen in Portland anymore. *Mixing in* is another term, meaning the same, but usually referred to only by Hispanics. *Jumping in* is a black term."

"You used the term *OG*. What does that mean?"

"An OG is an *original gangster*, because he has been around a long time, is the *shot caller* and has a lot of influence on others, especially the younger members.

"A key concept to the gang membership is to not show or be disrespected," Crannell continued. "A second key concept is to have power or *juice*. Respect is *very* important, and *dissing* could occur to you or someone close to the gang. Being dissed can actually cause the *dissee* to shoot the *dissor*."

"And what does it mean to *put it on the set*?"

"To *put it on the set* is equal to saying that 'I swear it is true' or 'Cross my heart.' If a person swore or put it on his set and did not follow through, he would be dissing himself. To put it on the set is not done lightly."

"What's the primary purpose of a gang?"

"To communicate fear," Crannell answered simply. "Fear is power, and power is obtained through violence, such as shooting."

Throughout all of these questions pertaining to definitions and gang activities, Mary was nodding her head, totally in agreement with everything Crannell was saying.

"How do you track gangs in Portland?"

"Well, we have a data base with the gang members' names."

"Does the gang name 'Sonny' come up in your data base?"

"No, it doesn't."

"Now Larry Martin stated that Beau Flynn told him that when he was fourteen, he had been jumped into the Portland Crips."

"Extremely unlikely," Crannell testified, "to the point of absurd."

"Why?"

"Because fourteen is too young, and a fourteen-year-old white boy being inducted into a black gang just stretches the imagination."

"In other words, Beau Flynn as well as Mary Thompson were making up their connection to these gangs?"

"Yes."

Skelton reached underneath the lectern for a paper cup filled with water. After taking a short draught, he continued.

"How does one come to control a set?"

"Control of a set comes from the territory claimed in its area, in other words, where gang members live and do business. Black gangs have territorial attitudes. Most others do not. The bottom line to a set is money."

At the defense table, Mary nodded.

"If there is no money involved," Cranell continued, "they could not care less about what the other sets do."

"Would someone from Portland, as Mary Thompson claims, be sent to take care of a Eugenean?"

"Unless it has to do with money, they would not care. To say that Portland gangs were watching this matter in Lane County, and then would send someone to kill Aaron Iturra, sounds like someone making it up."

Michaud smiled.

"Now what about this initiation, or jumping-in ceremony, with a stopwatch, the way Mary Thompson told her gang it was done?"

"Initiating someone in a ritualistic fashion probably would not happen, especially with a stopwatch. Nor is it a ritual to hand out do-rags afterwards to the newly initiated. I've never heard of it being done before, because as members become accepted, they just wear the rag, and it can be done even before they are really recognized as a true member of the gang. The jumping-in ceremony in Eugene was way more highly orchestrated than any I've ever seen or heard of in the past."

"In other words, Mary Thompson was manipulating these kids toward her own ends?"

"Objection!"

"Sustained."

"No further questions. Your witness."

"Were the films *Boyz N the Hood* and *Colors* artistic interpretations of gangs?" Chez began.

"I guess. I'm not a movie critic."

"Are gangs over-romanticized than they really are?"

"Well, I'm out there with the real thing every day and I have little time to go to the movies."

"Wasn't there some sort of mass media that dealt with a jumping-in?"

"Maybe a PBS special would have."

"How about 'Banging in Little Rock,' an HBO documentary?"

"Didn't see it."

"Is there an excitement at being shot at or shooting at someone?"

"I'd say that there is quite an adrenaline rush."

"Why do kids want to be *wannabes*, that is, pretend to be affiliated gang members?"

The implication was that the Eugene 74 Hoover Crips were not real gang members, and therefore not really that dangerous. Crannell would have none of that. He replied, "If kids are engaged in the same illegal, criminal activities, regardless of their affiliation, they are gang members.

"If you act like a gang member, claim you are a gang member, wear the clothing, do gang activities, then you are a gang member."

Does the phrase, Walk like a duck, quack like a duck, etc., ring any bells? Michaud thought.

"And if an activity, like murder, was done for the set, that would make it a gang crime," Crannell continued.

"Are there any white Crip gang sets?" Chez wondered.

"Some in California," Crannell replied.

At the defense table, Mary passed Chez a note. He looked at it.

"Is there a benefit to being a Crip over being a Blood?"

"No."

Mary looked down, disappointed with the reply.

"How do gangs derive their income?"

"Selling crack cocaine is the main source of money. Prostitution takes too long to make money. Narcotics are the fastest way to do it. Robberies are another good source of revenue."

Mary kept writing Chez notes. Apparently, the defense attorney was having trouble fathoming how gangs operated.

"Could we compare the West Coast gangs, the Bloods and Crips, to the Sharks and Jets of New York?"

Never mind that the Sharks and Jets were fictional, the names of the rival gangs in *West Side Story*. Crannell decided to give the question a serious reply to show how off the mark Chez really was.

"In the movie *West Side Story*, the Sharks and Jets used chains, knives and fists. The Bloods and Crips use *guns*—Uzis [Israeli-made machine pistols] and other types of automatic weapons that are far deadlier."

"What about the Dalton Gang of the Old West?"

A strange non-sequitur. Had Chez checked his facts, he would have discovered that the Dalton Gang rode in broad daylight to commit robberies—they never shot anybody in the back of the head the way contemporary gangs did. The other major difference was that the Daltons' reign of terror didn't last very long, a mere few years. Modern gangs saw their lifespans in decades.

"Are we making too much out of gangs?" Chez asked.

"No, we need the pressure on them. Gangs commit major crimes," Crannell testified.

"No further questions." Chez sat down in frustration.

All his cross-examination did was bolster the prosecution's case.

JUNE 26

"The state calls Lisa Fentress."

Two years before, when the murder took place, Lisa Fentress had been an adolescent. Now, she was sixteen years old and looked older in a light-colored suit, with long dark hair to her shoulders, and piercing eyes. She strutted to the stand like she owned the place.

In a soft, calming voice, she recounted how she'd telephoned Aaron to make sure he was home, then phoned Mary to tell him he was, and then called Elstad. "I called Jim and told him Aaron was home and to go do it and page me when it was done," she testified under direct examination. Her beeper had awakened her the next morning at 5 a.m. The digital display showed that she'd gotten a call from Mary the previous night at 1:40 a.m. She called Mary, who answered immediately. "She said that Aaron was taken care of. I asked if he was dead and she said, 'Yes.' She seemed happy."

"Did you ever discuss killing Aaron Iturra at Mary Thompson's home?"

"I recall sitting with Jim Elstad in Mary's living room and talking about different ways to kill Aaron."

"Was Mary Thompson in on those conversations?"

"She was always nearby, close enough to hear, if not participating."

"Do you recall anything she might have said about killing Aaron, specifically a preferred method?"

"I remember her saying, 'If you stab someone in the kidney, they'll bleed to death and won't be able to scream.' She said that once she'd went over to Aaron's house and hid in the bushes with a butcher knife, but wasn't able to do anything because Aaron left with some friends."

"Did she describe how she was dressed on that occasion?"

"She said she had on a hooded sweatshirt and Beau's blue bandanna on her head."

Skelton wanted to know why Elstad, once he agreed to do the killing, would actually go through with it.

"She reminded me that Jim had sworn on his set that he'd do it that weekend." And, of course, he did.

"Why did you initially agree to set Aaron up, Lisa?"

"Well, I was angry with him. Aaron was a snitch. But it was mostly because it made Mary so unhappy what Aaron was going to do about testifying against Beau." The last thing she wanted was for Mary, whom she idolized, to be unhappy.

"And did Mary reciprocate your feelings?"

"I thought Mary cared about me," she said with sadness. At the defense table, Mary, too, looked like she would cry.

On cross-examination, Chez immediately went to work attacking Fentress's credibility. "What kind of criminal background do you have, Ms. Fentress?"

Lisa admitted that she had bought a .22 caliber handgun from Mary for $65 in cash—a bargain in today's market—and some marijuana. She had also sold knives and drugs, and engaged in burglary, scrawling gang graffiti and plotting Aaron's death. It was a series of admissions designed to destroy her credibility as a witness. Then Chez went for the jugular.

"Did you make a deal with the prosecutor for your testimony?"

She said that yes she had, that in return for immunity from all charges arising out of Aaron's death, she had agreed to testify against Mary. "But that's not why I took the deal," she continued. "Testifying is the least I owe Aaron's family. I don't care if I go to jail."

Her testimony ended with tears as she buried her face in her hands and the judge recessed court for the day.

JUNE 27

"The state calls Larry Martin."

Larry "Truth" Martin, nineteen years old, took the stand. Wearing a shirt and tie and wire-rimmed glasses, his hair neat and slicked back, he looked more like a "yuppie" than a gang member.

He proceeded to testify that he had assisted Mary in burning gang photos and gang-style poetry she had apparently written celebrating Aaron's death. Mary told him ". . . not to put it in so fast because the flames [in her fireplace] were getting real big. She got scared the cops were going to search her house," said "Truth" under oath. He also said that he had used drugs with Mary regularly, from late 1994 to early 1995, before she was arrested.

Before the murder, he had heard Mary say, "He needs to be dead." She referred to Aaron with profane names in front of the kids who hung out in her place. She said that she wanted him "taken care of."

"Did you intend to kill Aaron?" Skelton asked.

"I did. I said I'd take care of Iturra, meaning I'd kill him. I didn't intend to go through with it, though, but figured it'd calm everybody down if they thought I was going to do it."

He said that the .38 used to kill Aaron was the weapon that he, Brown and some friends had stolen from a trailer home the week before the killing, that the gun had passed through the hands of many members of the gang, till it finally resided in his possession. Jim Elstad came to his house and took the gun on October 2. After he used it to kill Aaron Iturra, Elstad offered it back, and "Truth" categorically answered, "No."

Which made a lot of sense. What idiot would want to accept possession of a murder weapon after the fact?

Under cross-examination by Chez, Martin admitted that he was high on methamphetamine when he testified, falsely, to the grand jury, but that his testimony in court now was true and sober.

"Why should anyone believe your story now?" Chez asked.

"I'm out of that [gang] thinking. I'm done with everything that pertained to what happened in the past. I'm trying to go on with my future and have a better life."

Truth did admit that he used drugs so heavily in the period before and after Aaron's murder that his recollections were hazy. But, he added quickly, he stood by his current testimony. If it was a performance it was a good one.

"Are you sure it wasn't house-cleaning?" Chez asked, referring to the burning of the gang poetry and such in Mary's fireplace.

"I'm positive," Truth answered. "It was kind of like a panic thing."

Chez was improvising; Mary kept writing him notes during the cross-examination, from which Chez seemed to be drawing his questions.

"Do you blame Mary Thompson for your criminal past [that included breaking into cars and houses]?"

"No, I blame myself. But my friendship with Mary didn't help. I was in trouble and I stayed in trouble.

The trouble didn't stop," once he started hanging out with Mary. It escalated. He said that Thompson was a heavy drug user who smoked dope, snorted methamphetamine and popped pills.

"How do you feel about Mary Thompson now?" Skelton asked.

"I don't like her and I don't hate her. She's just a person."

Over the course of the next week, Skelton finished up his case. He had Ric Raynor testify about how Mary had, he maintained, gotten sucked into the gang life style, and how he'd warned her against the quicksand she found herself mired in, the quicksand of the power she had over the teenagers in her gang. Michaud testified about how the case was put together.

Jurors heard many of the taped calls between Mary and Joe Brown, then in custody, in which Brown responded to pressure from prosecutors to testify against Mary. "I'm going to tell them for the third time that I'm going to plead the Fifth because they won't let me testify for you," Brown told her during one of the conversations that Michaud and Rainey had listened in on.

"I don't know what they expect you to tell them," said Mary.

"I don't know anything. I can't remember anything," responded Crazy Joe. "I didn't do nothing wrong that I can think of, anyway."

"I love you," said Mary.

"I love *you*," Joe responded.

On the calls, all collect to Mary's house, Mary could be heard panicking over the continued police investigation, using profanity extensively to describe her continued persecution by police and, in particular, Michaud. Sometimes she would cry, sometimes she would be frightened, but always, always, she maintained that she had nothing to do with Aaron's murder.

Maybe it was just a question of telling a lie long enough and you believe it, Michaud thought. *Maybe she really doesn't think she caused the kid's death. Maybe she does have a conscience and she just couldn't deal with it if it was true. And maybe my brain is rotting and I'm just full of it.*

Finally, on July 10, after five weeks of testimony, the state rested their case. Now, it was the defense's turn.

FOURTEEN

PART OF STEVE CHEZ'S strategy for the defense was to use Joe Brown's own words to clear Mary Thompson. But that became difficult when Brown, in refusing to testify, was cited for contempt. Chez was then forced to play for the jury Brown's videotaped interview with cops at Aaron's house four days after the crime, when he reenacted the murder. In the tape, Brown says that, while Mary Thompson said that "she'd really love to see Iturra dead," he interpreted her words to mean that someone should "put the fear of God" into Aaron. It was left for the jury to determine what that meant.

Chez was making a valiant try, but he didn't have much of a defense. The prosecution tapes and witnesses had been particularly damning. The only thing that might persuade the jury to see reasonable doubt and therefore acquit his client was to have her testify. Of course, that was a dual-edged sword; the prosecution would get a crack at her too. But they had no choice.

JULY 11

This was it, the highlight of the trial, "Gang Mom" herself testifying. Would Chez be able to turn the tide that seemed to be moving inexorably against his client?

Or, would Skelton march forward and take her apart?

"Do you, Mary Thompson, swear to tell the truth, the whole truth and nothing but the truth, so help you God?"

"I do," Mary said, and sat down in the witness box. Michaud noticed that she had dressed for the occasion. She was wearing the same blue pants outfit for the second day in a row. Blue—her gang color.

Chez began with the basics, establishing that Mary was married to John Thompson, that she'd lived in Eugene approximately eight years, and in southern Oregon before that, that she had gotten interested in gangs due to the criminal involvement of her seventeen-year-old son Beau Flynn, whose criminal behavior first surfaced in 1992, and that her talks with Chuck Tilby, one of Eugene's two gang cops, sparked her further interest in gangs. She needed to know why Beau was attracted to gangs.

"What caused you to think Beau Flynn was interested in gangs?" Chez continued.

In a slow, sincere tone of voice, Mary said that things began to feel wrong around her house. She got wind that Beau was committing crimes. Then there was his school locker, painted on the inside with gang graffiti.

"Did you find a gun?"

"Yes, in his bedroom in a box of baseball cards."

Baseball cards? Michaud wondered. *Those are worth money. Why'd he bother to steal?*

Mary said that she had called Ric Raynor after finding the gun. By that time, Beau was already in jail for the first time.

Mary's allegiance to Raynor was making the cop's life difficult in the department. Many saw him as too sympathetic to a woman they believed to be a stone-cold killer.

"Did you subsequently get involved with gang members?"

"Yes, on the mall. They all had a story to tell. I would talk to them. Some were Beau's friends, some weren't."

"Do you know gang signs?"

"Yes," Mary said, and proceeded to sign some of them for the court.

"Where did you learn the signs?" Chez wondered.

"All over," Mary replied obliquely.

"From Aaron Iturra?"

"Yes."

So that's his strategy, Michaud thought. *Discredit the victim and the jury comes back with a "not guilty."*

Chez went on to establish Mary's anti-gang credentials as a member of the Gang Prevention Task Force. She was recruited, she said, by Officer Chuck Tilby, the same guy who was quoted in the *Register Guard* story as saying, "We need a hundred more like her" about Mary.

"What were your duties in the task force?"

"Gang prevention in Lane County, attending meetings, working on efforts to make a bus banner saying 'Don't let gangs make a killing here.' Also made T-shirts. I also attended a downtown conference on gangs."

"Do you know gang members?"

"Yes."

"What gangs are here [in Eugene]?"

Mary listed them by name: Crips, Bloods, Asian Pride, Latino sets. She was a sort of sociologist, interested in the whole concept of gangs. "I became obsessed, to get my son back." Books, documentaries, gang conferences, corresponding with police and juvenile authorities in San Francisco and Los Angeles, Mary became a real gang expert.

"Do you know what *mixing in* means?"

"Yes."

"How did you know?"

"I watched a documentary about it."

"Was Beau jumped in?"

"Yes, he told us some time later."

"Were Joe Brown and Jim Elstad jumped in?"

"I have no knowledge of them jumping in."

"Was Beau Flynn ever incarcerated?"

"Most of his young life."

"Was Beau in MacLaren in 1994?"

"He had been released."

"Was he home?"

"Yes."

"Were his friends at the house when he was home?"

"Yes."

"Who?"

"Larry Martin, Wayde Hudson, Jim Elstad, Joe Brown."

"Was the house a magnet [for gang members] when Beau was home?"

"Yes, when he was home, and away."

"How did you feel about that?"

Mary had no problems with the gang members hanging out at her place. She knew that if they were at her house, then they weren't out committing burglaries. In the interests of protecting the community, "They would talk and I would learn from them. I didn't judge them for their gang activities. They needed somewhere to be where they were able to be themselves."

"Did you walk the walk?"

"Yes."

"What does that mean?"

"I can talk the gang lingo, do gang signs, but I'm not really sure what *walk the walk* means. Beau would do this little thing, this little dance when he talked about his crimes. I guess that was it."

A regular Fred Astaire.

"Were you promoting or discouraging gang activity?"

"I'm not against gangs, I'm against gang violence. I don't want them to hurt people. I was able to intervene with the police."

"Did you have Beau arrested?"

"Many times."

"Did you turn kids in for having arms?"

"Yes, I would call Tilby or another officer."

"In 1994, after Aaron Iturra's death . . ."

"I knew very little about Beau's crimes prior to the death. After the death, Beau was released to me."

Then, despite the tapes the jury had heard, Mary gave an impassioned defense of Beau's character. How he "tried to do the right thing and then would try to deviate. He was brutally honest about his crimes. He started to hook up with the wrong people."

Skelton was on his feet in a flash.

"Objection, hearsay."

"I'll allow it to explain Ms. Thompson's activities," said the judge.

"Beau got no greater high than stealing while people were asleep. It's his rush in life, how he gets his high. I made a deal with him to not do any more crimes until after Christmas and then another one to stay clean until after New Year's, then we made daily deals to try to keep him home. He enrolled in Lane County Community College."

Beau Flynn, college boy. What would he do to a professor who didn't give him a good grade? Intimidate him? Burglarize his house? Shoot him?

"Do you know Wayde Hudson?"

"I met him through Aaron Iturra in 1994."

"Was he in your house?"

"Yes."

"Larry Martin?"

"I met him through Aaron Iturra in 1990."

"Joe Brown?"

"We met in, 1993 or 1994. I'm not sure when."

"Jim Elstad?"

"Same as Wayde."

"Angel Elstad?"

"I met her the Friday before Aaron Iturra's death."

Not according to Angel, who'd previously testified she had gone over to Mary's house ten or twenty times prior to the crime.

"Linda Miller?"

"I met her downtown on the mall in '92. Beau was on the run and I met her while looking for another gang member who might know where Beau was."

"Cameron Slade?"

"I met him through Aaron Iturra in 1994. He wasn't a frequent guest at the house. I didn't care for him much."

So now it's Aaron that's the common link between all these gang members, thought Michaud. *What, is this like the Kevin Bacon game on the net?* Pick any actor in Hollywood and you can find a way they are linked to Bacon. Only in real life, pick any gang member, Mary was asserting, and chances are they got into the gang because of Iturra.

"Who were the gang members?"

"Joe Brown, Aaron Iturra. Linda Miller claimed she was. Claimed she knew Tupak Shakur, the famous gang rapper. Only Beau was a Seventy-four Hoover. After Beau was arrested, Wayde, Joe and Jim claimed to be Seventy-four members."

"Lisa Fentress?"

"I met her at a gang-prevention meeting. She claimed membership in [another gang,] Sir Thirteen."

"How about other affiliations?"

"Seventy-four Hoover, not sure, maybe December or after Aaron Iturra's death."

"Are you a member?"

"No."

Liar, Michaud thought.

"You're not a Seventy-four Hoover member?"

"No."

Liar.

"You're not the leader of the Seventy-four Hoovers?"

"No."

Liar.

"Was Larry Martin at your house in late '94, early '95?"

"He lived there. He had issues at home and stayed at our house."

"Was Aaron Iturra at your house before September?"

"A lot. Weekly."

"Were Elstad or Brown?"

"Every so often with Wayde."

"Did you have a dispute with Aaron Iturra?"

"Yes."

"Over what?"

"Beau was arrested at Willamette High School. Beau was handcuffed in one room and Aaron Iturra in the other. Officer Grimes stated that Aaron said he took Beau's knife to keep Beau from hurting anyone. I was upset. I didn't think Beau stabbed anyone 'cuz he said he didn't. I couldn't believe Aaron was lying."

It was a mystery why Skelton hadn't objected. Whatever Grimes said to Mary was hearsay.

"Did Aaron look out after Beau?"

"I didn't ask him to," answered Mary, ducking the question. "Aaron Iturra told Beau they would hang out and do it right. I thought that Aaron could be a positive influence. He had risen above gang life. He was a talented artist. He was dealing with his issues and had a goal. I thought Aaron was above all this. I felt that Beau needed someone to go to. I felt all of us were honest with each other."

Now there's a mind-boggling concept, thought Michaud. *Mary Thompson and honesty.*

"Did any of the kids say Beau did the Grocery Cart?"

"No."

"Did they say anything different happened?"

Mary proceeded to say that it was Aaron who really had the knife, that Wayde, who was also there, got a hold of it somehow, and "Wayde said he had the knife but didn't think he stabbed anyone."

"Did you turn the knife in?"

"Yes."

"Where did you find it?"

"In Aaron Iturra's jeans piled up in the corner of Beau's closet."

"Were Aaron Iturra's clothes at your house?"

"Yes."

"What else?"

"His school stuff, backpack, clothes."

"Did you return his stuff to Aaron Iturra's house?"

"Yes, there was quite a bit. I gave it to Tina. I later asked Aaron if he took the knife from Beau. He said no, he said he took it from Wayde! We argued about Grimes's questioning at the high school. Aaron Iturra lied because Beau lied," Mary said, and started crying.

What a great performance.

"I was hurt. I changed my opinion of Aaron Itura." She continued to cry.

"Did you say negative things about Aaron Iturra to the kids?"

Michaud leaned forward.

"Yes, I was hysterical after Beau's arrest. Beau told Wayde to tell the truth. I paged Martin and Wayde. Larry called back and said he'd find Wayde. Then a pickup came and all these kids piled out. They were very upset. They said they can't believe Aaron Iturra lied. I told them all he had. I cussed him and said I wished he were dead. I made the statement September sixteenth, after the arrest."

"Any other statements?"

"Yes, I said I wish he were dead. Me, Joe and John were present."

"Any more negative statements?"

"None to that magnitude. I refused to have his name spoken in my house."

"Any of the kids say anything negative about Aaron Iturra?"

"No."

"Any kids threaten to kill Aaron?"

"Joe and Wayde in a group setting."

"Did *you* ever say Aaron Iturra needed to be taken care of?"

"No!"

The tapes, of course, contradicted her. But one thing for Mary—she was giving it her best shot.

There followed a series of questions about Mary's current and past drug usage. She testified that she didn't currently inject meth or snort it, or for that matter, smoke pot. Who knows? If she was asked if she had ever used pot, she might have answered, "Yes, but I didn't inhale." Then, to prove his client wasn't a saint, Chez asked if she had ever used drugs and Mary answered truthfully, "Yeah, at different points in my life."

"What is your house policy regarding drugs?"

"They could come to work through their problems, I wouldn't hide them. I respected them and they had to respect me by following the rules. No drugs. I wasn't running a flop house. They had to leave if they had drugs but could come back without them."

This despite the fact that gang members testified that they shared drugs with Mary.

"Alcohol?"

"It was not allowed in the house except for one occasion, when Beau was released and they were determined to get smashed, so I bought them some to drink at home."

"Ever inject meth?"

"Yes, in late April 1988 in southern Oregon. Hadn't

used it prior to that for some time. I was an informant."

Well, for a change, an honest answer.

"Did you have contact with the kids after your dog Lars died and before Aaron Iturra's death?"

"Yes, with Larry, Joe, Angel and Jim. Jim and Angel said they were going to Mapleton to kill a woman who'd abused her child."

Those in the courtroom listening had to wonder why, if there was even only a kernel of truth in that statement, she hadn't called Raynor or Tilby immediately.

"Did they have a gun?"

"Yes, Joe did."

"Where did the gun come from?"

"Joe Brown stole it in a burglary."

"Did the kids talk about the Pleasant Hill burglary?"

"Yes, there was talk all summer about a gun store in the country that didn't have an alarm system. Joe Brown wanted to do it. The weekend of Beau and Aaron's arrest, I learned it was in Pleasant Hill. I said they couldn't or they would get caught and go to jail. I told them it was federal mandate that all gun stores have alarms hooked into the police department. But gang youth always have a story, each badder than the one before. I thought they were just talking."

"Did you order any guns?"

"No."

"Who did?"

"Jim, Joe, Wayde, Angel."

"After that, did you see Angel with a gun?"

"Yes."

"What kind?"

"Blue Smith and Wesson thirty-eight."

"Did you touch it?"

"No, it was stuck in Jim's pants."

"Was it loaded?"

"No, they needed to buy bullets."

If she never touched the gun, how did she know it wasn't loaded?

"I told Jim to give the gun to Larry," Mary continued, "because he was more responsible. Jim was playing with it. Angel had it the next morning for the thing in Mapleton."

"Did you believe that she was going to shoot a woman in Mapleton?"

"No."

Despite the fact that the gang members were making threats, despite the fact that they were walking around with a gun, *Mary Thompson*, Michaud thought, *in her infinite wisdom, didn't believe they'd go through with it*. Just like she didn't believe they'd go through with killing Aaron.

"Any other contact [with the gang members]?"

"Jim called and said he swore on his 'hood that he would get Aaron Iturra. I asked him if he meant his set, not his 'hood, and he said yes. I told him to let the Portland gang member take care of Aaron Iturra. They were the ones who had issue with him."

The testimony of the Portland gang expert, Neil Crannell, completely contradicted what now appeared to be the cock-and-bull story that Mary had made up about "Sonny," the mysterious gang avenger from Portland.

"Did you feel there was any danger to Aaron in regard to Jim?"

"No."

"Joe had the gun, did you feel he was any danger to Aaron Iturra?"

"No."

"What happened next regarding Aaron Iturra?"

Mary told the same story she'd told the cops about Brown and Elstad coming to her house after the murder, confessing what they'd done and how she helped Joe dispose of the murder weapon, even though she thought it all some sort of charade.

"Did you think they'd killed him?"

"No, I couldn't believe it."

"Did Joe tell lies?"

"Yes. I went home and told John, and John said, 'It's just another story, Mary.' EPD was in the living room in the morning when I got up. They said Aaron Iturra was shot. They asked if I knew who did it. I asked them where Beau was. I thought maybe Jim and Joe were covering for Beau."

"Did you tell EPD what you knew?"

"No, I said there was a man at the house the week before that may have something to do with it."

"Was that true?"

"Yes." And Mary proceeded to tell the jury about "Sonny." This time, she embellished it a little. "He came in and said he needed to know about Aaron Iturra. He asked where he lived and if I had a picture. He said he wanted to see what Aaron Iturra did to Beau. I was evasive because I didn't know him. He was well-dressed but had no ID."

A well-dressed gang member? What, do they dress up when they're going out to do "hits"? And the bit with the ID. A "gang avenger" comes to your door and you ask him for his ID? Not likely.

"Were these other people real or a fantasy?"

There was a long pause.

She's pausing while she makes up her story, Michaud thought.

"I told the EPD about other people who had conflict with Aaron. I tried to get more information about the gun. EPD said it was a small caliber. I was trying to decide if Jim and Joe really did it. Beau was at Mac-Laren. I thought maybe some other kids that were having trouble with Aaron earlier in the week did it."

"Ever go to the police?"

"I went to the police and told them what I knew about Aaron Iturra. For three days I tried to put pieces together."

Michaud could see it now. A new TV series—'Mary Thompson, Private Eye."

"I wanted to make sure Beau was safe," said the concerned mother. "Angel came over and showed me the baby, and I asked her if she knew and she said Jim did it. I called Ric Raynor and left a message. He was at MacLaren talking to Beau and I wasn't comfortable talking to any other officers. I had a responsibility to tell what I knew. John and I went to look at puppies. Then I went to get Raynor."

And Mary related how she met Raynor, her friendly cop, and subsequently gave her statement to police.

"After Aaron Iturra's death . . ." Chez began to fumble, forgetting Joe's name. Collecting himself, he continued, "Did you have any communication with Joe?"

"Yes, I had daily conversations with Joe."

I'll bet that's not all!

"Did you discuss the murder?"

"Joe did. He got angry and said I wouldn't believe him anyway. I tried to get Joe to go to the police. Asked him to talk to Raynor, but he refused."

"Any communication with Jim?"

"He called Monday about Angel's baby. I asked him if Aaron Iturra was in the hospital dying and he said he wasn't aware of it. I asked if he shot Aaron and he said he wouldn't talk on the phone."

"Any further communication with EPD after the sixth?"

She had called Raynor in November. Seemed that someone was harassing her, through phone calls and letters mailed to her house.

"Anyone question you about your involvement in the murder?"

"Raynor, at my house."

"Did you know that you were a focal point of the investigation?"

"I thought that I had hindered it because I waited so long to tell the police what I knew. I became aware on October seventh that I was a suspect. I retained legal counsel."

"And was that me?"

"Yes, you advised me to keep in contact with the kids, but not to talk to EPD, except to tell them about the harassing notes."

So, now, Mary the *stoolie* was back. Only this time, she was willing to rat on kids to save her own behind.

"Did your attitude towards EPD change?"

"Yes, it changed drastically after Beau's arrest. The investigation was biased."

Then Mary related her version of the chase.

"On the seventeeth, Beau went to get the gun away from Lisa. He felt she might use the gun on herself or someone else." So Beau was trying to prevent a suicide attempt, rather than use the gun for criminal purposes.

"Lisa wanted a claim to fame. She changed daily. She wanted to shoot someone, deal drugs. Commit suicide. I don't care for that attitude."

"Did you know the Suburban was stolen?"

"Yes."

"How did you know?"

"Sam Warthan showed up in it. I asked where they got it and he said his uncle who worked at the DMV. Beau told me it was stolen and they had switched the plates. They were using the Suburban to get a gun. My Volkswagen wouldn't start."

"Did you attend a jumping in?"

"No."

Liar.

"Did you pick up Lisa at home on the twenty-fifth," and take her to the gang induction ceremony at the park?

"No."

Liar.

"Take the kids in John's truck?"

"No."

Liar.

"Give the kids bandannas?"

"No."

Liar.

"When you went to the police on October sixth, what did you feel your responsibility for Aaron Iturra's death was based on?"

"I hadn't paid enough attention to what the kids were saying or doing. If I had, he wouldn't have died," Mary said, and started crying.

Scripted tears, spare me!

"How did you feel?"

"I felt terrible." Mary continued to cry.

"Why don't we take a recess," Judge Velure broke in, "so the witness can collect herself?"

After the recess, Mary took the stand again, looking more composed.

"On October sixth, you told your concerns to the EPD?"

"Yes."

"What were your feelings for Aaron Iturra at the time of his death?"

"I was still a little bit angry. I thought about calling him after Lars died. I was resolved to being over the anger and hurt."

It was interesting. Mary used popular therapeutic terms like "issues" and "resolution," and yet, of anyone in that courtroom, she probably had more unresolved "issues" and less "resolution" in her life than anyone else.

"Did you intend anything you said to hurt Aaron Iturra?"

"No!"

Liar.

"Encourage others to hurt Aaron Iturra?"

"No."

Liar.

"Encourage others to beat up Aaron Iturra?"

"No."

Liar.

"Encourage others to kill Aaron Iturra?"

"No," Mary answered, and again began to cry.

Scripted! Liar!

"Are you glad they killed Aaron Iturra?"

"No."

She neglected to point out that with Aaron dead, there was no one to testify against Beau, and that Beau had been released right after the boy was murdered.

"Can anything you said be interpreted to mean 'Go kill Aaron Iturra'?"

"No."

Liar.

Mary continued to cry. *Wouldn't want to break the momentum!*

Chez turned to Skelton. "Your witness." Skelton got up to do the cross.

Skelton had been looking forward to this moment since the trial began. In most murder cases, the defendant doesn't take the stand because they become too vulnerable. But Mary had, and now it was the people's turn.

Unlike "Matlock," defendants rarely, if ever, confess on the stand. In fact, as soon as one did confess, the judge would stop the proceedings to give the defendant her rights and advise her against saying anything more until she consulted with counsel. In other words, the judge would make sure the defendant kept her mouth shut.

The reality was that, to impeach the testimony of a witness, you had to trip them up in their own lies, show them to be a liar, all in front of a jury. It was no mean task, especially with a system-savvy defendant like Mary.

Go get her Steve!

"Did you ask Sam to take the fall for the theft of the Suburban?" Skelton began.

Mary said that she believed Sam was responsible for the theft of the Suburban, and she was worried that Sam was gonna "snitch."

"Are you denying your son did the stabbing at the Grocery Cart?"

"Beau never admitted that," she answered cagily.

"You had the police report and the list of witnesses, right?"

"A partial list."

"You knew Larry was there?"

"Larry told me."

"When?"

"Right after Beau was arrested."

"You were concerned about Beau's participation?"

Mary's number-one concern, she said, was getting the truth out, that Beau had had nothing to do with the Grocery Cart stabbing, that it was all Aaron's fault. She was desperate to get this message out, because "Beau had several charges pending," and would go back to jail if convicted of the stabbing. But Mary's mission was repeatedly forestalled. She kept asking Larry Martin to go forward with the truth, and he kept refusing.

"Even though Larry *wasn't even there?*"

"Yes, he was a gang member."

"Did you finally persuade him?"

"He decided on his own."

Yeah, right.

"While Lisa was [at your house] did you make derogatory statements about Aaron Iturra?"

"Yes, Lisa and Joe did. There was name-calling."

"Such as?"

"Asshole, f---er, punk, mark."

"Did you make the statement 'Snitches get killed'?"

"Not in front of Lisa."

"To anyone?"

"Didn't Detective Rainey say that?"

"I'm asking the questions here! Are you saying that you never said that?"

"I don't remember telling Detective Rainey that he was a snitch." She did say that Aaron had lied in his statement to police.

"The question was, did you say 'Snitches get killed'?"

Mary sat on the witness stand as though she had wax in her ears. She just refused to answer.

"You aren't gonna answer the question?"

"I remember Detective Rainey said, 'Snitches get killed' " she finally answered.

"Did you ever say anything to Lisa that would make her conclude that you had made that statement?" Skelton asked, getting disgusted.

Mary muttered something. She was obviously stalling for time. But time had run out.

"Would the court make her answer?"

"No," Mary answered finally.

"If you didn't say anything, then why the statement during one phone call, 'If you don't tell, I won't tell'?"

"On the phone, Lisa said that. Lisa said some things after Aaron Iturra's death and the statement pertained to that."

End of the day, the saga continues tomorrow, stay tuned for more riveting action.

FIFTEEN

JIM "MR. BLACKWELL" MICHAUD noted that, for the third day in a row, Mary wore the same blue outfit. Her gang color admittedly, but couldn't she at least buy a new dress?

During the night, Skelton had carefully gone over his cross examination. For his part, he was determined to show Mary up as a liar on the stand.

"Well, Mrs. Thompson, you've had overnight to think about it. Regarding any conduct that you may have had with Lisa Fentress that was incriminating against Aaron Iturra, did you come up with anything else?" Skelton began.

"No," Mary replied.

"Your October sixth statements to the police were complete disclosure, is that correct?"

"Yes."

"Open the tape transcript to Number six-fifty, January twentieth. You are talking to Lisa about a police proposal that she take a polygraph. You say you don't think Lisa could answer any questions about you or she would fail. Why worry about it if you gave complete disclosure on October sixth?"

"We had talked since then and I believed her. I felt it incriminated me for not telling the police."

"Oh, you'd talked since then. So how would that incriminate you?"

"Because I didn't tell the police about her meetings with Wayde, Jim, Joe to do things to Aaron."

"Why does that incriminate you?"

"Because I didn't tell. I had forgotten about her, I didn't know her involvement."

"How could you be hurt if Lisa had immunity?"

"We weren't talking about immunity, we were talking about the polygraph."

"She passed the polygraph because she told the truth about you."

"She didn't tell the truth."

"Linda was only at your house a few times?" said Skelton, changing the subject to Linda Miller.

"The Friday prior to the death."

"What activities were incriminating towards Linda?"

"None."

Skelton went back to the prosecution table and, with a flourish, picked up the notebook that contained the wiretaps. It had already been marked off to a preassigned page.

"I call your attention to call Number six-forty-one, regarding the conversation between you and Linda. Wayde was called a snitch and you told her, 'I kept you out of it.' What did that mean?"

"I said I didn't hear her, not that she wasn't a part of it, so I kept her out of it."

"In your EPD statement to Rainey, you admit to calling Aaron Iturra names?"

"Yes."

Skelton flipped pages.

"Page three-forty-seven of the transcript."

Mary eyed him intently. What kind of trap was he setting?

"What do you mean when you say, 'I have to watch what I say, due to Crip nation. I am concerned for my son's safety and my husband's safety'?"

"They are all up and down the West Coast. Sonny from Portland was here, also TJ and Snoop."

"And they had some responsibility for Aaron's death?"

"They could have."

"You knew Jim and Joe were convicted already and you still believed Portland was responsible?"

"In an indirect way. Jim and Joe did it to get the proper respect from Portland."

"From people that don't exist?"

"They do exist."

"How would you incriminate Portland?"

"By talking in court like I am now."

"They monitored your calls?" Skelton asked sarcastically.

"No, they read the papers."

"Why worry if you have no gang connection?"

"I'm connected through my son."

"Wasn't your son in MacLaren at the time?"

"Yes."

Skelton then reviewed the history of the Aaron Iturra/Beau Flynn friendship, leading up to the incident at the Grocery Cart.

"If Aaron and Beau were friends, why retaliate, why not let Aaron Iturra tell the truth at Grand Jury about what really happened?"

"I hoped he would."

"Your reaction was to get angry, et cetera."

"Yes."

"*In fact, he was gonna tell the truth about Beau and you wanted to eliminate him as a witness, isn't that true?*"

"Objection! Argumentative," Chez yelled.

"Objection sustained," said the judge.

But Skelton had gotten the question in, directly implicating Mary in the plot to kill Aaron and the jury was not going to forget that.

"What negative things did you say to Wayde about Aaron Iturra?"

"I called him names, said 'I wish he were dead,' said 'I can't believe he hurt me,' said 'He couldn't testify.' "

"When did you say those things?"

"After Aaron and Beau were arrested, the next day."

But she later changed, realizing that her remarks could be misinterpreted when taken out of context, and told Wayde, "I said leave Aaron Iturra alone."

"Anything else?"

"I don't remember anything. I may have called him a 'buster.' "

"What was the context of the remark, 'Leave Aaron Iturra alone?' "

"They were talking about beating him up."

"The last message from you to Wayde was 'Leave Aaron Iturra alone'?"

"Yes."

"Did Wayde make negative statements against Aaron Iturra?"

"I don't recall any statements Wayde made. I don't believe he would have."

"Wayde was a Seventy-four Crip?"

"I was told some of them had become Seventy-four Crips."

Calling on Mary's expertise, Skelton asked how many Seventy-four Crip sets there were in Eugene. Mary answered, "One that Beau formed in Eugene," and that "there were other members in it."

"Who?"

Mary thought for a few moments. "*Doug Edwards.*"

Mary wouldn't respond further to the question. She seemed conflicted.

"Your Honor," Mary asked politely, "can I speak to my attorney?"

"No," the judge came back hard, "answer the question."

"*Fred Johnson, Jace Turner, Lyle Bolander* and *Ted Carington* and some I know by their gang names only."

"In your statement to police, you denied knowing anything [about a gang] or guys you thought were just wannabes. That's not true, huh? There were actually members of the set?"

"Yes."

"Now, Jim Elstad called and said he swore on his 'hood to kill Aaron Iturra. Did you take it seriously?"

"I didn't believe him."

"Would you take someone else seriously?"

"I took Beau seriously."

"If these were members of Beau's gang, why not take them seriously? What makes it serious?"

"The person saying it."

"On October third, if you didn't think Jim and Joe were serious, even though they came to your house after killing a boy, what harm was there in telling the police?"

Mary began to hedge and talk in circles.

"Would the court please instruct her to answer?"

"Mr. Skelton, please read the question again," the judge ordered.

Skelton repeated his question.

"It would cause great harm to tell the police the truth. I was concerned for my son."

"What harm could come to Beau in MacLaren if you told the truth?".

"I was trying to protect Beau."

"From what?"

"Maybe Beau had told Jim and Joe to do it."

"Did you intend to lie to EPD when you told them Jim and Joe did it?"

"I didn't believe it."

"Was the other part of the statement a lie too?"

"I diverted the police, but it was not intentional," Mary said.

Michaud noticed that for the first time, Mary didn't sound so confident. Her con was unraveling in front of her like a loose ball of thread. She had no place to turn but to, ironically, the truth.

"If you didn't believe Jim and Joe did it, then why drive to the river?"

"He didn't take the bullets out in my truck."

"Did you tell him to throw it in the river?"

"I said to go do it," Mary admitted.

That was something she hadn't said before. *Now, she's implicated herself consciously in the conspiracy*, Michaud thought.

"The gun was involved in the homicide?"

"True."

"You insisted he throw out the gun?"

"Yes."

"How often did Jim and Joe come to your house and admit they did the shooting?"

"Once."

"How often after you said to shoot Aaron Iturra?"

"Once."

Mary had goofed and didn't realize it, just as she had when she admitted to setting the whole thing up to Janyce.

"You expect this jury to believe you didn't believe them?"

"Yes."

"Were you afraid for your own life, of Jim and Joe?"

"Yes."

"Were you in fear at the river?"

"Not at that time, after EPD was at the house and I had a chance to think about it."

"How come Joe called you 'Moms'?"

"I knew him a lot of years, he just did it on his own."

"The others?"

"They picked it up from Joe."

"Out of affection for you?" voice dripping sarcasm.

"Yes."

"Did Jim and Joe say they did it for you?"

"No!"

"So you didn't have to worry anymore?"

"I don't remember it."

"What did they say?"

" 'We shot Aaron Iturra.' I said, 'Who?' They said, 'Jim did it.' I said, 'Did you really do this?' They said, 'Yeah.' I didn't believe them."

"What techniques did you use of power and control?"

It was a rather sophisticated question. Skelton was getting to the heart of gang violence: the ability of the leader to control and manipulate those around her to do her bidding.

Mary answered, "I talked to them, I didn't control. They did what they wanted to do. I tried to discourage them."

"You didn't do anything to control them?"

"I lied about the gun store alarm," she said, referring to their plan to steal guns, and how she allegedly stopped them with her cock-and-bull story about the federal mandate that all gun stores have alarms hooked into the police department.

"You would lie to them?"

"Yes. I would tell them the truth too."

"The kids would confide in you, and EPD would ask your opinion, just because you talked to them?"

"Yes."

Skelton changed the subject. Mary was getting comfortable. He had to get her dancing again.

"How did Lisa become a Seventy-four? What would cause her to become a Seventy-four?"

"Involvement with people associated with the Seventy-four."

"She was your friend?"

"Yes."

"She was a fourteen-year-old female, all the rest were males?"

Mary nodded.

"If Lisa was your friend, how was she acquainted with the others?"

"Through Aaron Iturra."

"You had no role in her Seventy-four membership?"

"No."

"You have a history of drug use?"

"Yes."

"Going back to the gun, you sent Beau to get it, right?"

"I did not send him."

"You sent him to get a gun from Lisa."

"It was Beau's plan and I agreed."

"You knew Beau wanted the gun to do a burglary?"

"No, I thought that once Beau got the gun it could be disposed of."

"You thought the gun was safer with Larry than Joe?"

"Yes."

"Under your direction," Skelton's voice rose, "you thought it was safe to put a gun into the hands of a seventeen-year-old drug user?" Skelton marshaled the most incredulous expression he could muster.

"Yes."

"Instead of taking it or calling the police?"

"Lots went through my mind."

"Do you feel it is proper for gang members to have a gun in your house?"

"Not normally, there was a lot going on."

"On the reenactment tape, Joe said, 'Mary wanted Aaron Iturra dead.' "

"I said leave him alone."

Is that sweat I see on your forehead, Mary?

"Part of the plan was to tell you after it was done. What part of the plan were you involved with?"

"No part of the plan."

It was a weak rejoinder, and a denial that appeared to be much, much too late. But then again, you could never tell with juries. Look what happened with O.J. in L.A. Slam dunk case and Bam! the guy walks.

Skelton had finished. After a perfunctory redirect by the defense that went absolutely nowhere, the defense rested. Closing statements followed, then the judge charged the jury. After eight hours of deliberation, they came back with their verdict.

SIXTEEN

WEDNESDAY, JULY 17, 1996
8:58 p.m.

FOR A WHILE, SOCIAL scientists and others were looking to explain away the aberrant behavior of criminals by saying that they had lousy backgrounds. It worked for awhile, until the apologists started getting mugged themselves and suddenly, they weren't apologists anymore.

The jury knew nothing of Mary Fockler's background, that she had been the apple of her father's eye, that she had had a mother who'd stroked out, another brother who tried to commit suicide and crippled himself, and that she herself had served in the military, albeit briefly. If they had, would they have considered that information in their verdict?

Even had the facts of her earlier gang life with the Hells Angels been known at the time, which they weren't, they could not have been presented to the jury. Never mind that it established a pattern of gang activity going back twenty years. Jurors may only consider the evidence in front of them. What Mary Thompson or Fockler or whatever she wanted to call herself had done during her earlier life was totally irrelevant. Whatever problems she had that led to her criminal behavior were also irrelevant. At least legally.

As the jury filed back into the box, Mary looked over, trying to read the verdict on their faces. Good luck; she might just as well have been trying to read the faces on Mount Rushmore. The jury wasn't giving it away by expression.

"Ladies and gentlemen of the jury, have you reached a verdict?"

"We have, Your Honor."

"Would the defendant please rise?"

Mary Thompson rose to her feet with her attorney Steve Chez beside her.

"What say you on the matter before this court?"

"We, the jury, find the defendant, Mary Thompson, *guilty* of aggravated murder."

They don't believe me!

Stunned, Mary dropped her head.

In the front row, Janyce Iturra breathed a heavy sigh of relief. Then her thoughts turned heavenward. "Rest easy, my son."

"Take the defendant into custody," said the judge. "Sentencing on July twenty-third."

Big, beefy bailiffs surrounded Mary and snapped on handcuffs and leg irons. Shuffling off, she looked back and saw Michaud. For a moment, their eyes locked. He nodded, the most emphatic, self-satisfied nod in the history of law enforcement.

Six days later, on July 23, 1996, Judge Lyle Velure was ready to pronounce sentence on Mary Thompson. Mary came shuffling back into the courtroom. One more time, it remained for Janyce Iturra to get in the next-to-last word in her victim's impact statement to a hushed courtroom.

Relating for the last time the drama of her son's death, the tragedy of the situation was lost for some in the repetition of events. But when Janyce looked at Mary and said quietly, "Who could hurt a child like this?" everyone, including the hardened court personnel, listened.

"We asked God, Why have you done this to us?" Janyce continued, "We've always done the right thing. Why us?" But the Almighty didn't answer. His answer, she said, was Aaron's death.

Mary looked down and shook her head.

Since their home was still a crime scene, returning there was not an option. Instead, "We went to a friend's house and the first thing I did was call Mary Thompson to let her hear from me what had happened. I didn't want her to hear of Aaron's death on the TV or radio. She was Aaron's friend. I needed to let her know. I must have tried ten times that day. She never called me back. By the next day I gave up, knowing by this time she already knew. I kept saying, 'I'll see her at Aaron's funeral, she'll be there, she's our friend. She cared for Aaron.' The defendant always talked about how Aaron was such a good kid and was going to make it."

Now she knew that was all a con. Now she knew why Mary had distanced herself: she had ordered Aaron's death.

As for Mary's so-called anti-gang activities, "The defendant is evil personified. Why? Because she took in children, purporting to love and protect them. She gave them a place to just be themselves and then, when they were the most vulnerable, used them for her own gain."

The idea that the kids called Mary 'Moms' "makes my skin crawl. From where I am sitting, a mom is someone who takes responsibility for her actions and her children's." Mary, clearly, did not.

"All the Defendant did as a mother was try to cover up her son's actions by lying and, beyond belief, even murdering my son, my children's brother. The main difference between you and me, Mary, is, somewhere along the line you forgot the entire idea of parenting."

Throughout the trial, one question never seemed to be answered: was Mary a con woman from the beginning, as Michaud believed, or did she gradually succumb to the power of gangs, as Raynor believed? To Janyce, the answer was now obvious.

"You had no real intention to prevent gang activities. You were active in manipulating the system so Beau wouldn't get caught. All a very big cover-up. First at Aaron's expense, but also Beau's other friends': Joe, Jim, Lisa, Cameron, Larry, Linda, and all the rest."

Had Mary not been caught, she never would have been stopped. The reason, Janyce said, was, "You enjoy the rush it gives you to be the mastermind and still be able to undermine the system. You played the game too well, thinking in your distorted mind that you would never get caught." But, of course, she had. "The defendant has no feelings or true connections with other people, especially her so-called friends. The defendant is a manipulator and controlling person."

In her grief Janyce might actually have settled on the truth about Mary. There's one school of sociological thought that says the endorphin rush from pulling a job is what keeps criminals in the game. They are more addicted to that "high" than they are to the actual criminal behavior. In fact, being psychopaths, not feeling the way normal people do, that high is the only way they can feel at all.

"But these young adults, through this entire process, are now beginning to realize they are somebody and they are worth more than you ever gave them credit for. They should be applauded for taking the courage to step back to look, and to own their own part in this. The willingness to turn their lives around, to be productive, respected people in this community."

Then Janyce turned to the physical and emotional toll the death had on her and her family.

"At one point in time, I was taking stomach medicine, sleeping pills, anxiety pills and depression medication and pain pills. All I take now is anti-depression medication, just to keep me on an even level to make it through each day, and medication to help allow me to get some sleep. You must know it's not a given anymore. Just until recently I couldn't even think of sleeping without going through all the elements of that night and how it affected me and my family."

She related how she, her daughters and her son were all in therapy to cope with Aaron's loss. Maya, in particular, was having problems.

Maya still felt responsible for Aaron's death. She was the one who took the set-up call from Lisa. No longer able to cope with that guilt, Maya took what she hoped would be a fatal mixture of drugs and alcohol in January 1996. She survived, but, "This brought more overwhelming expenses: ambulance, emergency room and drug treatment—the effects of murder just are neverending. The counseling does not come free. We exhausted all benefits through my insurance for the next two years. What is left over after bills are paid, I try to pay what I can on these expenses."

Even Aaron's death cost the family financially.

"The cost of Aaron being in the hospital on October third, from two a.m. until he died at ten forty-five was over twenty-two thousand dollars, not including ambulance and doctor fees. The bill from the hospital was waiting at my home after I and my family returned from staying at a friend's home." The bill for Aaron's funeral alone was six thousand dollars.

As the money was depleted, so were the friendships. "Friends abandoned us because of their own fears. We felt diseased, like there was something wrong with us. Yet we were the homicide survivors."

Mary shook her head.

"Considering all of this there is only one appropriate sentence for Mary Thompson: death. I understand that this is not possible under the law, but she has taken so much from us all. If she gets life in prison, at least that will guarantee that she will not hurt anyone else."

Janyce sat down. No one said a word for a moment and then the judge broke the silence.

"Mary Thompson, please stand," he intoned.

Mary stood. Judge Lyle Velure sentenced Mary Louise Thompson to spend the rest of her life in prison with no chance of parole.

After the sentence was rendered, the bailiffs snapped the leg irons and handcuffs on. It was "Gang Mom" who had come into the courtroom to hear the sentence; it was just another two-bit convicted murderer who was led shuffling away.

Outside the courtroom, Lisa Fentress was waiting. She went up to Janyce, looked into her eyes for forgiveness and collapsed crying in her arms.

"Oh, what can I do, what can I do?"

"Just live a good life." And Janyce too began crying.

That evening, Jim Michaud stood on the porch of his home. It was an unusually clear night and there wasn't a cloud in the sky, just stars as far as the eye could see. He looked up and felt good. He'd done a good job. That was the intrinsic. As for the tangible, in one hand he had a perfect martini that he sipped, in the other, Paula, whom he had since married. They began to kiss and soon, they walked arm in arm into the back bedroom.

And then the phone rang.

AFTERWORD

AS THE MILLENNIUM APPROACHES, Oregon's prisons have begun to burst at the seams. To alleviate the problem, the state has arranged with Arizona to take some of their inmates. Mary Thompson is one of those. She currently resides in a prison someplace outside Phoenix, Arizona.

Beau Flynn has a scheduled parole hearing during 1998. It is not expected that he will get out, but Janyce Iturra is concerned.

Janyce and her kids are doing all right. Some still go to therapy and every year around the time of Aaron's death, they get sad. But they carry on as best they can.

Under a new plan by Eugene's chief of police, all detectives are supposed to be rotated back to uniform. Les Rainey was one of the first to go. Jim Michaud, though, appears to be safe for a while.

While the 74 Hoover Crips are no longer active in Eugene, gang crime in the town continues to be a problem, with no solution in the foreseeable future.

ACKNOWLEDGMENTS

Many people helped in the writing of this book. In particular, I'd like to express my appreciation to my editor Charles Spicer who allowed me to develop my voice; Gary Sledge, my editor at *Reader's Digest* who first saw the potential in this story; Jim Michaud, who gave everything and expected nothing; Janyce Iturra who allowed me a privileged glimpse into the lives of her and her family; and Sara, who helped me with structure many mornings during 2 a.m. feedings.

AUTHOR'S BIOGRAPHY

Described in Tom Byrne's book, "Writing Best Selling True Crime and Suspense," as a "mover and shaker" in investigative journalism, Fred Rosen is the best-selling author of "Lobster Boy."

"Gang Mom" is currently being developed into a TV movie by *Reader's Digest*. The *Digest* recently asked Mr. Rosen to investigate the most infamous murder in the history of Charlotte, NC, that will be the subject of a future article in the magazine.

A former columnist for *The New York Times*, Mr. Rosen taught journalism at Hofstra University for seven years. He is currently an Adjunct Associate Professor of Communications Arts at The New York Institute of Technology.

SHE LOVED HER SONS...TO DEATH.

Hush Little Babies

THE TRUE STORY OF A MOTHER WHO MURDERED HER CHILDREN

DON DAVIS

Not since the Susan Smith case has a murder so shocked the nation: a beautiful, loving mother is horrified to find her two young sons stabbed to death on her living room floor by an intruder. Hearts go out to poor Darlie Routier, who appeared to live for her children. But overwhelming evidence soon finds Darlie, the neighborhood's "Most Wonderful Mom," guilty of slaying her own innocent children in cold blood...

HE STOLE THEIR HEARTS—THEN TOOK THEIR LIVES...

SMOOTH OPERATOR

THE TRUE STORY OF SEDUCTIVE SERIAL KILLER
GLEN ROGERS

Clifford L. Linedecker

Strikingly handsome Glen Rogers used his dangerous charms to lure women into the night—and on a cruel date with destiny. For when he got them alone, Rogers would turn from a sweet-talking Romeo into a psychopathic killer, murdering four innocent women during a six-week killing spree that would land him on the FBI's "Ten Most Wanted" list. Finally, after a twenty-mile high speed police chase, authorities caught the man now known as one of history's most notorious serial killers.

SMOOTH OPERATOR
Clifford L. Linedecker
___96400-5 $5.99 U.S./$7.99 CAN.